KEN BURNS

with **DAVID BLISTEIN** and **CAULEY POWELL**

★ ★ ★ ★ ★ ★ ★ ★

A TREASURY OF AMERICAN PRESIDENTS

GROVER CLEVELAND, AGAIN!

★ ★ ★ ★ ★ ★ ★ ★

Illustrated by **GERALD KELLEY**

ALFRED A. KNOPF · NEW YORK

For my daughters: Sarah, Lilly, Olivia, and Willa
And my grandchildren: Lyla, Finn, and Jax
Presidential timber all
—Ken Burns

THIS IS A BORZOI BOOK PUBLISHED BY ALFRED A. KNOPF

Text copyright © 2016 by American Documentaries, Inc.
Jacket art and interior illustrations copyright © 2016 by Gerald Kelley

All rights reserved. Published in the United States by Alfred A. Knopf, an imprint of Random House Children's Books,
a division of Penguin Random House LLC, New York.

Knopf, Borzoi Books, and the colophon are registered trademarks of Penguin Random House LLC.

Visit us on the Web! randomhousekids.com
Educators and librarians, for a variety of teaching tools, visit us at RHTeachersLibrarians.com

Library of Congress Cataloging-in-Publication Data
Names: Burns, Ken. | Kelley, Gerald, illustrator.
Title: Grover Cleveland, again! : a treasury of American presidents / by Ken Burns ;
  illustrated by Gerald Kelley.
Description: New York : Knopf Books for Young Readers, 2016.
Identifiers: LCCN 2015043443 (print) | LCCN 2015046579 (ebook) | ISBN 978-0-385-39209-9 (trade) |
  ISBN 978-0-385-39210-5 (lib. bdg.) | ISBN 978-0-385-39211-2 (ebook)
Subjects: LCSH: Presidents—United States—History—Juvenile literature. |
  Presidents—United States—Biography—Juvenile literature.
Classification: LCC E176.1 .B9346 2016 (print) | LCC E176.1 (ebook) |
  DDC 973.09/9—dc23
LC record available at http://lccn.loc.gov/2015043443

The text of this book is set in 15-point FlingaLing Regular.
The illustrations were created using pencil and digital color.

Printed in the United States of America
July 2016
10 9 8 7 6 5 4 3 2 1
First Edition

★ ★ ★ ★ ★ ★ ★ ★

A NOTE FROM KEN BURNS

I have four daughters—Sarah, Lilly, Olivia, and Willa. When they were little and had trouble falling asleep, I would recite the names of the presidents to them. (Yes, that's a historian's idea of a lullaby!) After a while, they knew the names so well, we turned it into a memory game. We'd start with our first president and work our way up. I'd say "George" and they'd say "Washington"; I'd say "John" and they'd say "Adams." Their favorite part was when we got to Grover Cleveland, the only president who had two *non*-consecutive terms. I'd say "Grover" and they'd say "Cleveland"; I'd say "Benjamin" and they'd say "Harrison"; then I'd repeat "Grover" and they would giggle and say "Grover Cleveland, again!" I vowed to my oldest, now a mama of her own, that one day I'd do a children's book on the presidents called *Grover Cleveland, Again!* It's been almost thirty years, but I've kept my promise.

Unlike my children, I didn't memorize the names of all the presidents as a child, but even in elementary school, history was my favorite subject. Then, when I went to college, I met a remarkable documentary photographer and filmmaker named Jerome Liebling. He showed me how a single still image could make history come breathtakingly alive by revealing the *story* within the history. Ever since then, I've tried to use film—which is, basically, a sequence of individual images—to reveal the whole complex history of America. Much of my work focuses on the experience of everyday people, because looking closely at their pictures can tell us so much about life back when they were living. So, in this book, in addition to describing the important things that the presidents did when they were in office, I talk about who they were as *people.* After all, presidents have birthdays and brothers and sisters and even pets, just like everybody else! There are also fascinating stories of things that happened to them on their road to the presidency—stories that tell us a lot about their times.

How could someone who had never voted in an election become president? How could someone who had hardly ever gone to school keep the country from being torn in two? How could a man with dyslexia lead the country through a world war, and one with a serious physical disability guide us through another? How could the son of a peanut farmer bring together two countries whose people had been ancient enemies? This is amazing stuff!

Learning about American history might not teach a child how to become a famous scientist or the CEO of a major corporation. But it can make a huge difference in their lives. It certainly has in mine.

There's much in our history that doesn't make me proud: the great stain of slavery and the entrenched racism that still haunts us, the forced imprisonment of American citizens simply because of their ancestry, the myriad disparities in criminal sentencing that plague our judicial system, and—especially as the father of daughters—all the ways that women have so often been relegated to second-class citizenship. (Note: there are no women in this book . . . yet!) We cannot forget these mistakes. But we must also remember the very many qualities of our nation that are worth celebrating—in particular, our steadfast faith in the value of freedom and our fervent desire to right our wrongs. We shouldn't underestimate the ability of our children to understand these principles, nor the effect that understanding can have on their lives: from the causes they support and the candidates they vote for to why it's essential for us to be more tolerant of each other *and* our differences—which is, I believe, one of the most important things we can teach them.

I hope that, like my family, you enjoy getting to know Grover Cleveland and the forty-two other remarkable individuals who have held our nation's highest office—and that maybe, just maybe, your children will become as fascinated by our history as I am.

★ ★ ★ ★ ★ ★ ★ ★

GEORGE WASHINGTON

"Liberty, when it begins to take root, is a plant of rapid growth."

Official portrait by Gilbert Stuart

PRESIDENT: April 30, 1789–March 4, 1797

BORN: February 22, 1732

WHERE: Westmoreland County, Colony of Virginia

DIED: December 14, 1799 (age 67)

SISTERS: Elizabeth ("Betty"), Mildred, and a half sister, Jane

BROTHERS: Samuel, John, and three half brothers, Butler, Lawrence, and Augustine

OCCUPATIONS: surveyor, farmer, general, commander-in-chief of the Continental Army

VICE PRESIDENT: John Adams

PARTY: none

NICKNAME: "Father of Our Country"

WIFE: Martha Dandridge Custis Washington

CHILDREN: none of his own, but he was a surrogate father to his stepchildren, Jack and Patsy

PETS: seven dogs, a donkey, and a parrot; many horses, including Old Nelson and Blueskin. He also had sheep, pigs, and mules on his farm.

LOOK FOR HIM! $1 bill, 25¢ coin, Mount Rushmore

Americans call **GEORGE WASHINGTON** the "Father of Our Country." We do this for two reasons. He was the leader of our army during the Revolutionary War *and* he was our first president.

Washington never went to school but read and studied a lot on his own. He was especially good at math, and his first job was making maps. He also became a soldier in the Virginia Regiment. Back then, Great Britain and France were fighting over which country owned different parts of North America. We were still part of Great Britain, so Washington fought against the French. That's where he got his reputation for being a really smart and brave soldier.

So, when the colonies decided to fight for their independence *from* Great Britain, the leaders of the American Revolution selected him to be the commander-in-chief of the Continental Army. In fact, *every one* of the people in charge of the Revolutionary War voted for him.

He hoped to return to his farm after the war, but again he was asked to serve his country . . . this time as the president. Washington worked hard to keep the new states unified. Indeed, he's the only president who did not belong to a political party. He also started many traditions. For example, he gave a State of the Union address every year, chose his own Cabinet of advisers, and figured out a way for the president and Senate to make treaties with other countries. He served two terms (eight years), leaving office in 1797. By then he was sixty-five years old and happy to return to his farm in Mount Vernon, Virginia. Unfortunately, two years later, he died suddenly after falling ill during a long horseback ride in a bad storm.

A "LIE" ABOUT A "LIE"! There's a famous story that Washington chopped down his father's cherry tree and, in admitting it, said, "I cannot tell a lie." Actually, that story was a "lie" . . . something a writer made up about him. But he had a good reason. He wanted to give an example of how honest George was.

WOODEN TEETH? Another made-up story! His teeth *were* bad and he ended up wearing a fake set after his fell out. The false ones were made of ivory, animal teeth, and even human teeth! But not wood. Still, it doesn't sound like he brushed very well, which is strange because he had his horses' teeth brushed!

WAIT! ISN'T ENGLAND OUR FRIEND? These days, England is one of our *best* friends. But in George Washington's day, Americans were forced to obey King George III of England. We fought the Revolutionary War so we would be free to make our own laws and rules.

STATES? COLONIES? WHAT'S THE DIFFERENCE? The colonies were ruled by British law. Once the colonies formed their own governments after the Revolutionary War, they became states.

Most people are famous for being *first*. Not JOHN ADAMS. Even though he was the *first* vice president, he's more famous for being the *second* president. At the same time, he and his wife, Abigail, were the *first* president and first lady to live in the White House (which they called the Executive Mansion back then). In fact, it was so new they had to hang the wash in what is now called the East Room!

First or second, John Adams is one of the most important people in American history. After going to Harvard College, he became a lawyer and worked on his family farm, just down the road from Boston. He strongly believed the country should be free from England and was one of the five people who wrote the Declaration of Independence.

Many presidents are known for the wars America fought while they were in office. John Adams is known for the war we *didn't* fight. When he was elected president, England and France were fighting each other to see who could "own" the ocean. We were still a small country and didn't want to take sides, but we didn't have much choice. Both countries kept capturing our ships so the *other* side wouldn't get food and supplies from us. Most people thought we should fight France, but Adams secretly figured out how to make a deal with the French dictator, Napoleon. This was not a popular decision. He knew it meant he probably wouldn't win the next election. (And he was right. He came in *second*.) But he believed it was the right thing for America. He was so proud of standing up for what he believed, he asked to have inscribed on his tomb: "Here lies John Adams, who took upon himself the responsibility of the peace with France in the year 1800."

DON'T FORGET TO WRITE! Since he was away from home a lot, John and his wife, Abigail Adams, wrote more than a *thousand* letters to each other. Historians love old letters! They tell us a lot about what people were really thinking back then. For example, Abigail urged John to give women equal status with men in the Declaration of Independence. (If she had convinced him, it would have said "all men and women are created equal," the way most people think it should have!) Those letters are among the first examples we have of a woman arguing for equal rights.

JOHN ADAMS

"Posterity! You will never know how much it cost the present generation to preserve your freedom. I hope you will make good use of it."

Official portrait by John Trumbull

PRESIDENT: March 4, 1797–March 4, 1801

BORN: October 30, 1735

WHERE: Braintree, Massachusetts Bay Colony (now Quincy, Massachusetts)

DIED: July 4, 1826 (age 90)

BROTHERS: Peter, Elihu

OCCUPATIONS: lawyer, diplomat

VICE PRESIDENT: Thomas Jefferson

PARTY: Federalist

NICKNAMES: "Atlas of Independence," "His Rotundity"

WIFE: Abigail Smith Adams

DAUGHTERS: Abigail ("Nabby"), Susanna, Elizabeth

SONS: John Quincy, Charles, Thomas

PETS: dogs, including Juno and Satan, and a horse named Cleopatra

STAND UP FOR WHAT'S RIGHT. In 1770, a crowd of people started attacking British soldiers in Boston. The soldiers shot into the crowd, and five American colonists died. It was called the Boston Massacre. But lawyer John Adams agreed to defend the enemy soldiers because he believed everyone has the right to a fair trial. (He won the case.)

MY FAVORITE JOHN ADAMS STORY. Before the Revolutionary War, Congress met in Philadelphia. Since there were no trains or planes, Adams had to travel by himself from Massachusetts *on horseback*. That trip now takes about seven hours by car. It took Adams eight or nine *days*. And he did it more than once! That's how committed he was to America's freedom.

THOMAS JEFFERSON

"We hold these truths to be self-evident: that all men are created equal."

Official portrait by Rembrandt Peale

PRESIDENT: March 4, 1801–March 4, 1809

BORN: April 13, 1743

WHERE: Shadwell, Colony of Virginia

DIED: July 4, 1826 (age 83)

SISTERS: Lucy, Elizabeth, Martha, Anna, Jane, Mary

BROTHERS: Randolph, Peter Thomas, Peter Field

OCCUPATIONS: writer, inventor, lawyer, architect, statesman, farmer

VICE PRESIDENTS: Aaron Burr, George Clinton

PARTY: Democratic-Republican

NICKNAMES: "Man of the People," "Sage of Monticello"

WIFE: Martha Wayles Skelton Jefferson

DAUGHTERS: Martha ("Patsy"), Mary ("Polly"). He also had three daughters and a son who died in infancy.

PETS: two bear cubs; his horse, Caractacus; and a mockingbird named Dick

LOOK FOR HIM! Jefferson Memorial; 5¢ coin, which has his face on the front and the estate he designed, Monticello, on the back; $2 bill; Mount Rushmore

HE COULD MAKE YOUR HEAD SPIN! Among many other things, Jefferson invented the first chair that could spin around, as well as the lazy Susan, a rotating tray people can spin to get things like salt and pepper without reaching across a dining table. It's also great for playing Scrabble.

Ever wonder what you'll be when you grow up? How about a writer, inventor, architect, scientist, botanist, philosopher, musician, historian, and *president* of the United States? THOMAS JEFFERSON was *all* those things. And more!

When Jefferson was only thirty-three years old, he wrote the first draft of the Declaration of Independence. It includes a list of more than twenty-five ways in which the king of England was treating Americans badly. It also includes the five most famous words in American history: "all men are created equal."

Thomas Jefferson and John Adams had been good friends, but by the time Adams was president, they were enemies. Adams was a Federalist. He believed that the government in Washington should have more power to make laws for everyone. Jefferson was a Democratic-Republican. He believed the states should be able to decide most things for themselves. In the election of 1800, they fought as hard as any two people have ever fought to become president. It was close, but Jefferson won.

Then Jefferson did something surprising. He gave a speech that said, "We are all Republicans, we are all Federalists." Nobody roots for *both* teams in the World Series or Super Bowl, do they? But that's what Jefferson meant. No matter which political party you belong to, we all are "rooting" for America.

The most famous thing Jefferson did as president was to make an agreement with France to purchase the Louisiana Territory. It cost about $15 million. That sounds like a lot of money, but for around 3¢ an acre he had doubled the size of the United States. In fact, parts of fifteen states are now on that land, from Louisiana all the way to Montana.

Later in life, Thomas Jefferson and John Adams became close friends again and often wrote letters to each other about everything from current events to their memories of the Revolutionary War. But what's *really* amazing is that they both died on the same day—the Fourth of July, 1826—the fiftieth anniversary of their Declaration of Independence.

ONLY MEN ARE CREATED EQUAL? Did you notice that Jefferson said "all men" instead of "all people"? He didn't just leave out *all* women; he left out all the women *and* men who were slaves. He even owned slaves. He actually thought slavery should end, but it seems that he never *really* believed black Americans should be treated as the equal of whites.

WHAT'S OUT THERE? When Jefferson acquired the land of the Louisiana Purchase, it was largely wilderness. So he asked two men named Meriwether Lewis and William Clark to explore it, along with a crew of about thirty-five men and, later, an Indian woman named Sacagawea, who became one of the most famous Native Americans in history. The trip covered more than 8,000 miles—including 5,000 miles of unknown territory—and took more than two years. They did it all on foot, on horseback, by canoe, or by keelboat—no planes, trains, or automobiles. And they hardly even had a map!

NEWS DOESN'T TRAVEL FAST. The peace treaty ending the War of 1812 was signed in late 1814. But since it was signed way over in Europe—and they didn't have texting back then—a big battle took place a month later in Louisiana. The war was officially over, but not everyone knew it.

THE MEASURE OF THE MAN. James Madison was our shortest and lightest president. He was only five feet four inches tall and weighed about one hundred pounds.

JAMES MADISON

"If men were angels, no government would be necessary."

4

JAMES MADISON'S family was so wealthy from tobacco farming, he could have done whatever he wanted, but he loved to learn things, so he went to Princeton University.

After college, he spent many years as a public servant and, in a single summer (1787), helped to write the Constitution of the United States. That's the collection of rules that the president, Congress, and the Supreme Court still follow so they can do what they think is right for the *whole* country while also protecting the rights of every person. Madison's most important achievement was to suggest that Americans agree to a "Bill of Rights," which became part of the Constitution. It lists the ten freedoms that Americans should always have, including the freedoms to speak any opinion, practice any religion, and be treated fairly if accused of a crime.

Like John Adams, Madison had to try to keep the United States from getting in the middle of a war between France and Great Britain. Both countries were still capturing our ships to keep them from bringing supplies to the other side. Because Great Britain was even blocking our shores so our ships couldn't sail, Madison felt we had to declare war on them. This became known as the War of 1812. At first we didn't do very well. British soldiers actually made it all the way to Washington, D.C., and set the Capitol and the White House on fire. President Madison's wife, Dolley, had to hide in the woods for a few days until the soldiers left! According to legend, she saved the original Declaration of Independence from being captured by the British.

No one really won the war. But we finally signed a peace treaty with Great Britain. As bad as it was, the War of 1812 proved that Americans could put aside their differences when they needed to defend the country.

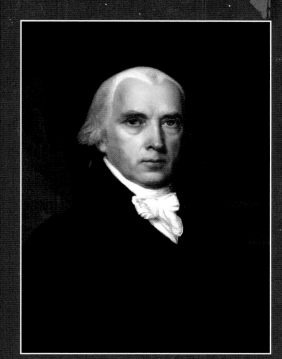

Official portrait by John Vanderlyn

PRESIDENT: March 4, 1809–March 4, 1817

BORN: March 16, 1751

WHERE: Port Conway, Colony of Virginia

DIED: June 28, 1836 (age 85)

SISTERS: Nelly, Sarah, Frances

BROTHERS: Francis, Ambrose, William. Five other siblings died when they were very young.

OCCUPATION: He worked in government his whole life.

VICE PRESIDENTS: George Clinton, Elbridge Gerry

PARTY: Democratic-Republican

NICKNAME: "Father of the Constitution"

WIFE: Dolley Payne Todd Madison

STEPSON: John

PET: a parrot named Macaw

LOOK FOR HIM . . . OR NOT! Madison's face was on the $5,000 bill until it was discontinued in 1969.

"OH, SAY, CAN YOU SEE?" When I was a kid, I always wondered what the national anthem was about. It turns out that an American named Francis Scott Key was negotiating a prisoner exchange on a British ship during the War of 1812. One night, he saw "the bombs bursting in air" as the British attacked an American fort. The next morning, he saw "that our flag was still there." Key was inspired to write a poem about that night. One day, someone sang it to the tune of a popular British drinking song, and pretty soon it became "The Star-Spangled Banner," our national anthem.

5

JAMES MONROE

"The best form of government is that which is most likely to prevent the greatest sum of evil."

Official portrait by Samuel Morse

PRESIDENT: March 4, 1817–March 4, 1825

BORN: April 28, 1758

WHERE: Westmoreland County, Colony of Virginia

DIED: July 4, 1831 (age 73) (Remarkably, three of the first five presidents died on the Fourth of July. The others were Adams and Jefferson.)

SISTER: Elizabeth

BROTHERS: Spence, Andrew, Joseph

OCCUPATIONS: soldier, lawyer

VICE PRESIDENT: Daniel D. Tompkins

PARTY: Democratic-Republican

WIFE: Elizabeth Kortright Monroe

DAUGHTERS: Eliza, Maria

SON: James

PETS: a spaniel named Buddy and a Siberian husky named Sebastian

JAMES MONROE was a really good student, but when the Revolutionary War began in 1775, he dropped out of college to fight for freedom.

After the war, he studied law with Thomas Jefferson and became very active in government. The people of Virginia elected him to be a United States senator once and governor twice. He was also secretary of state for President James Madison.

These experiences taught him how to help people compromise. In fact, one newspaperman called his presidency the Era of Good Feelings.

But those good feelings would not last long, because when Missouri wanted to become a state, there was a fight in Congress about whether it would be okay to own slaves there or not. Finally, Congress agreed that whenever a "slave state" joined the United States, a "free state" would have to be let in at the same time. So Maine got to come in as a free state when Missouri was admitted as a slave state. This was called the Missouri Compromise.

When Monroe was president, the government was just starting to figure out how banks should work. In those days, people wanted to borrow money to buy land. But land prices were going up and down so fast that many people couldn't pay the banks back, forcing some banks to shut down. That made people afraid of leaving money in banks, causing even more to shut down. It was called the Panic of 1819.

President Monroe is most famous for the Monroe Doctrine. This was a promise that we would protect any country in North or South America if they were ever attacked by a foreign country. It said to European powers that they couldn't have any more colonies in the Americas. That's when we began to become a major world power.

LET'S MAKE A DEAL. A lot of presidents have to deal with money and banking, which is a very confusing topic. In fact, many people would say, "You're too young to understand." I don't think you are. So let's try.

When I was a kid, if I had a little money, I "deposited" it in the bank. I always trusted the bank to have the money there when I needed it.

I didn't realize it back then, but the bank was lending my money to other people to buy things like houses and businesses.

Banks can get in trouble when they lend money to people who can't pay it back. This scares the people who have their deposits in those banks, so they try to take all their money out. That can cause people to panic. (Kids can get their money out no matter what.)

A BIG FIGHT OVER AN IMAGINARY LINE. To decide which states would allow slavery, the government went back to an imaginary line that Charles Mason and Jeremiah Dixon had drawn on a map many years before to settle some border disputes between colonies. It was called the Mason-Dixon line. The states below the line could own slaves. The Civil War would be a fight between people who lived above the line and people who lived below it.

SEND THEM BACK TO AFRICA? President Monroe had an idea that seems strange now. He thought that if slaves were freed, they should be given money to go back to Africa and make a country for themselves. Some former slaves did return and founded Liberia. They named the capital Monrovia in his honor.

GEORGE WAS STILL NUMBER ONE. Even though individuals vote for president, the final decision is up to a small number of people that each state sends to represent them. This is called the Electoral College (even though it's *not* a college and you don't learn very much if you're in it). In 1820, James Monroe came close to winning every vote in the Electoral College. Only George Washington had ever done that. One person voted for someone else, so George would stay number one.

JOHN QUINCY ADAMS was the first son of a president to become a president. People always include the "Quincy" in his name so it's clear they're talking about him, not his father, John Adams.

After the Revolution, his father made several trips to Europe to represent the United States, and John Quincy went with him. By the time he was fourteen, he had visited France, the Netherlands, and even Russia. So when he became president, he was very good at communicating with different countries to make agreements.

John Quincy Adams also believed that it was important for the government to do things that helped *all* the people in *all* the states. For example, he thought we should build roads and canals and bridges to make it easier to travel from state to state. But many people thought the government should only do what it *had* to do, like have an army or deliver the mail. People still disagree about which things the individual states should do and which ones the *United* States should do.

After John Quincy Adams was president, he planned to retire, but people in Massachusetts wanted him to be one of their representatives in Washington. So he went to Congress.

By then, people in Congress were arguing about slavery all the time. In 1836, the representatives from the South made a rule that nobody could even *talk* about slavery in Congress anymore. Adams was very opposed to slavery and knew how important it was to keep trying to find a way to end it. It took him eight years, but he finally got Congress to get rid of that rule.

He continued to do everything he could, until the end of his life, to make the United States a better place. In fact, he was working in Congress the day he had a stroke. He died two days later.

OUCH! John Quincy Adams kept his pet alligator in a bathtub in the East Room of the White House.

WHAT DID *YOU* DO YESTERDAY? John Quincy Adams always knew the answer to *that* question. He wrote in his diary every day from the time he was seventeen until he died. That's more than 20,000 days!

JOHN QUINCY ADAMS

"America does not go abroad in search of monsters to destroy."

Official portrait by Gilbert Stuart

PRESIDENT: March 4, 1825–March 4, 1829

BORN: July 11, 1767

WHERE: Braintree, Massachusetts Bay Colony (now Quincy, Massachusetts)

DIED: February 23, 1848 (age 80)

SISTERS: Abigail ("Nabby"). Two other sisters, Susanna and Elizabeth, died as young children.

BROTHERS: Charles, Thomas

OCCUPATIONS: lawyer, diplomat, professor, statesman

VICE PRESIDENT: John C. Calhoun

PARTY: Democratic-Republican. Belonged to other parties over the years.

NICKNAME: "Old Man Eloquent"

WIFE: Louisa Catherine Johnson Adams

DAUGHTER: Louisa, who died shortly after her first birthday

SONS: George, John II, Charles

PETS: an alligator. Also, his wife raised silkworms, and she harvested their silk to use in her gowns.

LIKE FATHER, LIKE SON. Just like his father, John Quincy Adams was elected president. Unlike his father, he didn't have the most votes. Four men had run and none of them had gotten more than half the votes. Finally, Congress had to make the decision. They chose John Quincy Adams.

THINK FOR YOURSELF. At different times, John Quincy Adams was a member of seven different political parties! The only thing he was "loyal" to was what he thought was right.

ANDREW JACKSON

"The rich and powerful too often bend the acts of government to their selfish purposes."

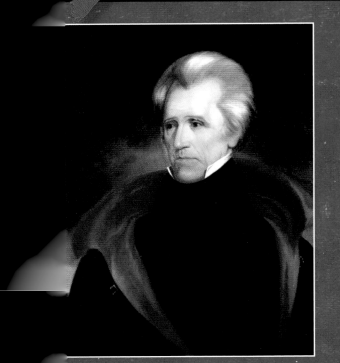

Official portrait by Ralph E. W. Earl

PRESIDENT: March 4, 1829–March 4, 1837

BORN: March 15, 1767

WHERE: the Waxhaws region, on the border between North and South Carolina

DIED: June 8, 1845 (age 78)

BROTHERS: Hugh, Robert (both were born in Ireland!). Five other brothers and sisters died when they were very young.

OCCUPATIONS: soldier, statesman, farmer

VICE PRESIDENTS: John C. Calhoun, Martin Van Buren

PARTY: Democratic

NICKNAME: "Old Hickory"

WIFE: Rachel Donelson Robards Jackson

ADOPTED SONS: Andrew Jr. and Andrew Hutchings (both his relations) and a Creek Indian orphan named Lyncoya (Andrew Jackson and his family were also the guardians of eight children. Four were Rachel's orphaned nephews; the other four were the orphans of a family friend.)

PETS: his horse Sam Patch, and a number of horses for racing, including Thruxton, Emily, Lady Nashville, and Bolivia. He also had a parrot named Poll.

LOOK FOR HIM! $20 bill (He was also on the Confederate $1,000 bill!)

Presidents like to say they are just ordinary people, but many early presidents were born to rich parents and lived on large, fancy farms. Not ANDREW JACKSON. He was the first person to become president who had been poor as a child. One reason rich people had always been elected before him is that you used to have to own property to vote. Now more states were letting people vote even if they didn't own a home. These new voters appreciated that Jackson (who gained wealth after growing up) knew what it was like to be poor.

Jackson was known as a populist. That means he believed laws should help ordinary people as much as rich ones. If Congress tried to pass a law he didn't think was fair, he wouldn't sign it. When the president refuses to sign a law, it's called a veto. Jackson never hesitated to veto a bill if he didn't like it. In fact, he vetoed more bills than all previous six presidents combined!

Jackson also wanted to make sure banks helped ordinary people as much as rich ones. Before he was president, most of the country's money was in one national bank. That bank was owned mainly by wealthy people who got to decide who could borrow money. Sometimes they made such bad decisions, many people lost a lot of money. Jackson thought it would be better if the money were kept in banks all over the country. That way, local people would have more control over who could borrow it. As we'll see, that idea worked, but not for long!

Andrew Jackson did a couple of things in particular that most people think were wrong. First, he strongly supported the institution of slavery. He also supported states that forced Indian tribes to leave their homes so there would be more land for white people. The courts said that wasn't right. Jackson ignored them. He said the Native Americans *did* have to leave. The path they traveled became known as the "Trail of Tears" because so many of them died from cold, hunger, and disease on the way. The United States promised the Native Americans that they would never be forced to leave their *new* lands, but that promise was later broken.

REMEMBER THE ALAMO! When Jackson was president, Texas was part of Mexico. The Texans wanted to be free and declared their independence as the "Republic of Texas" in March 1836. That started a war with Mexico. One of the first battles was at a fort called the Alamo. The Texans lost that fight (even though Davy Crockett was there!) but won the most important battle in 1836, the Battle of San Jacinto, and became independent. In 1845, Texas was admitted into the Union as the twenty-eighth state.

WHERE DO WE GO NOW? As a kid, Andrew Jackson was a practical joker. His favorite trick was to move people's outhouses (outdoor bathrooms) during the night so they couldn't find them.

WHAT A PARTY! You usually need a special invitation to go to an inauguration party. President Jackson opened the White House doors to everyone. Hundreds of people came in to shake his hand (and get some free food!). They made quite a mess, but it was a great party.

CUT THROUGH RED TAPE? Van Buren was well known for being able to help people "cut through red tape," an expression that means to get things done when there are lots of rules and regulations. I always wondered where that expression came from, so I looked it up! It turns out that in the old days, big stacks of laws and rules would be tied up in red tape. If you actually wanted to get something done, you had to cut through that tape and get right to the piece of paper you needed.

MARTIN VAN BUREN

"It is easier to do a job right than to explain why you didn't."

One of the hardest things about being president is that you often get blamed for what the president before you did. That sure happened to **MARTIN VAN BUREN**! Remember how President Jackson had allowed every state to have banks and make their own rules? Well, unfortunately, these local banks started to lend too much money . . . especially to people who wanted to buy land. The result was called the Panic of 1837. Van Buren never quite figured out how to fix it. That's one reason he wasn't elected a second time.

Although he never went to college, Van Buren had worked at his dad's tavern when he was growing up, where he learned a lot about people from all over the country just by listening to them talk when they stopped for the night. This made him very clever when it came to getting people to go along with his ideas. One time he even stopped the state of Maine from getting into a big fight with Canada over where their border was.

Another time, after Texas had declared its independence from Mexico, it wanted to become a state. But the "Republic of Texas" (as it was called then) was near the area of the country where people could own slaves. Van Buren was against slavery, so he found a way to keep Texas from becoming a state, until later.

Sometimes Van Buren might have been too clever! He'd find ways to get people to vote for him whether they wanted to or not, by doing special favors for them, like helping them get a job. In fact, he was so good at getting people to do what he wanted, people called him the "Little Magician" and the "Sly Fox." Soon politicians would do things like this all the time, but he was one of the first.

Official portrait by Francis Alexander

PRESIDENT: March 4, 1837–March 4, 1841

BORN: December 5, 1782

WHERE: Kinderhook, New York

DIED: July 24, 1862 (age 79)

SISTERS: Dirckie ("Derike"), Jannetje ("Hannah") (Van Buren also had one half sister from his mother's previous marriage.)

BROTHERS: Lawrence, Abraham (Van Buren also had two half brothers from his mother's previous marriage.)

OCCUPATIONS: lawyer, politician

VICE PRESIDENT: Richard Mentor Johnson

PARTY: Democratic. Belonged to other parties over the years.

NICKNAMES: "Sly Fox," "Little Magician," "Old Kinderhook"

WIFE: Hannah Hoes Van Buren (She died before he became president.)

SONS: Abraham, John, Martin Jr., Smith. Another son and a daughter died in infancy.

PETS: two tiger cubs! (They were a gift from the sultan of Oman, but Congress made Van Buren give them to the zoo.)

FREE SOIL PARTY? That sounds like a garden giveaway celebration, right? It's actually the name of a political party that wanted to stop new states from letting people have slaves. Eight years after Martin Van Buren left office, he became part of that party and ran for president again. He didn't win.

CAN YOU HEAR ME? Van Buren loved to sing loudly, particularly in church. His favorite hymn was "O God, Our Help in Ages Past," and by the time he was done singing, *everyone* knew it by heart! The song was sung at his funeral.

"The strongest of all governments is that which is most free."

REMEMBER TO WEAR YOUR HAT AND COAT. Some people say that Harrison died of pneumonia because it was a cold, snowy day when he gave his first speech as president (which we call the inaugural address). It didn't help that he wasn't wearing his coat or hat and gave the longest inaugural speech ever—almost two hours!

Official portrait by James Lambdin

PRESIDENT: March 4, 1841–April 4, 1841 (That's right . . . just one month!)

BORN: February 9, 1773

WHERE: Charles City, Colony of Virginia

DIED: April 4, 1841 (age 68)

SISTERS: Elizabeth, Anna, Lucy, Sarah

BROTHERS: Benjamin, Carter

OCCUPATIONS: soldier, government official (His dad made him go to medical school, but when Dad died, he dropped out and joined the army!)

VICE PRESIDENT: John Tyler

PARTY: Whig

NICKNAMES: "Tippecanoe," "Old Tippecanoe"

WIFE: Anna Symmes Harrison

DAUGHTERS: Elizabeth, Lucy, Mary, Anna

SONS: John Cleves, William, John Scott, Benjamin, Carter, James

PETS: a goat named Billy and a cow named Sukey

REMEMBER TO VOTE—AS SOON AS YOU CAN! In Harrison's election, eight out of every ten people who could vote did. These days, usually only five or six out of every ten people vote. You can register to vote as soon as you are eighteen. So do it! (Tell them I sent you!)

One month isn't a long time to do any job, especially the job of president of the United States. But that's how long **WILLIAM HENRY HARRISON** was in office before he became very sick and died. (Sad to say, that's the most famous thing he did while president.)

Harrison died so quickly that three people were president that year: Martin Van Buren (who was president just before him) and the new vice president, John Tyler, who became president when Harrison died.

Before he was president, Harrison was an officer in the army. He spent many years in what they called the Northwest back then, but we now call the Midwest. In 1801, he became "governor" of the Indiana Territory, an area that became Indiana, Illinois, Michigan, Wisconsin, and part of Minnesota. It also included the Great Lakes. That's a lot of land. And water!

Many people voted for Harrison for president because he was known as a "brave Indian fighter." That's because one of his jobs as governor of the territory was to protect settlers from being attacked by the Native Americans, who had lived there for centuries. The settlers became especially worried when Tecumseh, a famous Shawnee chief, began to convince several tribes to fight together to get their land back. (He hoped someday that they could have a separate "Indian Nation.") When these tribes attacked Harrison's army in 1811 at the Battle of Tippecanoe, the Americans won a decisive victory. And in a battle in 1813, Harrison's army would kill Chief Tecumseh, who is still known as one of the smartest and bravest Native Americans in history.

TIPPECANOE? Harrison was known as Tippecanoe because he won a battle against the Native Americans at Tippecanoe Creek in what is now the state of Indiana.

AND TYLER TOO? This was the first election where campaign slogans became popular. Since John Tyler was running for vice president with Harrison, their slogan was "Tippecanoe and Tyler Too." It's a famous phrase, but very few people (besides you and me) know what it means.

JOHN TYLER was William Henry Harrison's vice president. One of a vice president's main jobs is to be there in case the president dies. Since Harrison died just a month after becoming president, Tyler didn't have to wait long.

The problem was that this had never happened before, so no one knew exactly how it should work. Some people thought Tyler should stay president until the next election in four years. The people on the other side wanted a new election as soon as possible. Until then, they thought Tyler should just agree with everything Congress did.

Tyler liked the idea of staying president for all four years. And he didn't like the idea of agreeing with Congress all the time.

The people who didn't like him had another problem. Tyler wanted the states to be strong to protect people from being pushed around by Congress. As a slave owner, he especially didn't want Congress to pass a law abolishing slavery. He argued a lot with a senator named Henry Clay, who thought the United States government could do many things that would help *everyone.* For example, if the government had enough money, it could build roads and bridges and canals that connected many states. But that would mean more taxes, and Tyler didn't like that idea. Clay also thought that there should be one big bank again in Washington that would be more powerful than the state banks. Tyler didn't like *that* idea either. Arguments like this happen even today.

As a result, Congress kept passing laws and Tyler kept vetoing them. One important bill he signed into law let people buy 160 acres of government land cheaply. This was one of the main reasons so many settlers who had moved out west came to own their own land at last.

JOHN TYLER

"I can never consent to being dictated to."

DO YOU *STILL* REMEMBER THE ALAMO? Texas had wanted to become a state ever since the battle of the Alamo eight years earlier. However, since Texas was in the South—and covered a huge area—the territory would come in as one or more slave states. So Northern states stopped it. But Virginian John Tyler kept trying, and he got Congress to agree just before he left office.

PRESIDENT ROBIN HOOD? Tyler believed rich people should use their money to help the poor . . . just like Robin Hood. So he named his home after Sherwood Forest, the place where Robin Hood and his "merry men" hid out.

Official portrait by George P. A. Healy

PRESIDENT: April 4, 1841–March 4, 1845

BORN: March 29, 1790

WHERE: Charles City County, Virginia

DIED: January 18, 1862 (age 71)

SISTERS: Anne, Elizabeth, Martha, Maria, Christiana

BROTHERS: Wat, William

OCCUPATIONS: lawyer, politician

VICE PRESIDENT: none

PARTY: Whig

NICKNAME: "Accidental President"

WIVES: Letitia Christian Tyler (she died just a year after Tyler took office), Julia Gardiner Tyler

DAUGHTERS: Mary, Letitia ("Letty"), Elizabeth ("Lizzie"), Alice, Julia, Pearl. Another daughter, Anne, died very young.

SONS: Robert, John III, Tazewell, David, John Alexander ("Alex"), Lachlan, Lyon, Robert (That's *fifteen* children . . . more than any other president.)

PETS: his trusted horse, General; a pair of wolfhounds; an Italian greyhound; and a canary

HE DIDN'T PLEDGE ALLEGIANCE. Many years after he left office, Tyler took the side of the South during the Civil War. He is the only president who ever became an official "enemy" of the United States.

JAMES K. POLK

"The presidency is no bed of roses."

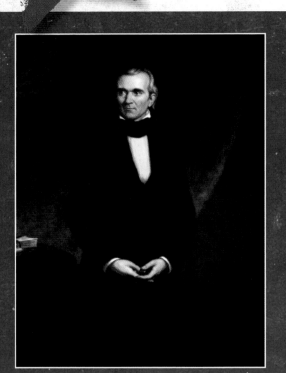

Official portrait by George P. A. Healy

PRESIDENT: March 4, 1845–March 4, 1849

BORN: November 2, 1795

WHERE: Pineville, North Carolina

DIED: June 15, 1849 (age 53)

SISTERS: Jane, Lydia, Naomi, Ophelia

BROTHERS: Franklin, Marshall, John, William, Samuel

OCCUPATIONS: lawyer, politician, farmer

VICE PRESIDENT: George M. Dallas

PARTY: Democratic

NICKNAME: "Young Hickory" (He had worked for—and learned a lot from—"Old Hickory," Andrew Jackson.)

WIFE: Sarah Childress Polk

WARD: Marshall, Polk's nephew

PETS: He had no official pets!

JAMES K. POLK may have been the hardest-working president of all time. He worked twelve to sixteen hours every day and didn't take a single vacation while president. He was so exhausted, he died from cholera just three months after leaving office.

One reason he worked so hard was that he tried to solve four big problems: (1) arguments with Canada and Mexico about where their borders were; (2) arguments in Congress about which new states could have slaves; (3) where to get the money to pay for everything; and (4) how to make sure the government took good care of that money.

Polk did a pretty good job with all of these problems. First, he helped reduce tariffs. A tariff is basically a tax on imported or exported goods, like food or clothing or machines. All tariffs make things cost more for some people and less for others. He not only made the tariffs fair, but he made sure the government took good care of the money by creating an independent Treasury to make rules about money instead of having state banks do it.

Finding solutions to borders and slavery was harder. In the Northwest, we almost had a border war with Canada. But he compromised, and we ended up signing an agreement that gave the United States the area that is now Oregon and Washington. On our southern border, Polk went to war with Mexico. In the end, we won and forced Mexico to sell us, for very little money, what is now California, Arizona, Nevada, Utah, and most of New Mexico. Through it all, Congress was arguing about whether we should be at war in the first place and, if we won, which territories would be slave states. . . .

No wonder Polk was so tired.

STANDING UP FOR DAD. James Polk's first case as a lawyer was to defend his father, who was accused of fighting in public. He got Dad off with a $1 fine.

I'LL NEVER DO *THAT* AGAIN. When James Polk ran for president, he said he would not run for re-election. And he kept his word. He is also known for keeping all his other campaign promises. I wonder what it would be like if every president were in office for just one term.

ARE YOU IRISH? While President Polk was in office, many people in Ireland were starving to death during what's called the Irish Potato Famine. As a result, hundreds of thousands of Irish immigrants came to America. A new political group, which came to be called the Know-Nothing Party, was started by people who thought America was letting too many Irish people come here.

LIGHTEN UP! Gaslights were first put in the White House while Polk was president. Before that, they only had candles and oil lamps.

23

A LONG, HOT DAY. On July 4, 1850, President Taylor had to sit in the hot summer sun for a long time listening to speeches during the Fourth of July festivities at a fund-raiser for the newly dedicated grounds upon which the Washington Monument was being erected. He ate cherries and drank milk to stay cool. The milk back then wasn't pasteurized and we don't know how fresh it was, plus the cherries were probably really sour. Anyway, he got very sick. He died five days later.

LEAVE OLD WHITEY ALONE! Taylor kept his warhorse, Old Whitey, on the White House lawn until he found out that visitors were taking horsehair as souvenirs.

GO FOR THE GOLD! When Taylor was president, gold was discovered in California. So many people went there, it was called the Gold Rush. More than 300,000 people came from all over the world hoping to "strike it rich"! At first, gold was easy to find by separating the larger gold nuggets from regular stones in the rivers. But soon it wasn't easy at all, and many people went home empty-handed.

ZACHARY TAYLOR

"I hope my real friends will never have to blush for me, so far as truth, honesty, and fair dealings are concerned."

Official portrait by Joseph Henry Bush

PRESIDENT: March 4, 1849–July 9, 1850

BORN: November 24, 1784

WHERE: Barboursville, Virginia

DIED: July 9, 1850 (age 65)

SISTERS: Elizabeth Lee, Sarah, Emily

BROTHERS: William, Joseph, Hancock. Two other boys died young.

OCCUPATION: soldier

VICE PRESIDENT: Millard Fillmore

PARTY: Whig

NICKNAME: "Old Rough and Ready"

WIFE: Margaret ("Peggy") Mackall Smith Taylor

DAUGHTERS: Ann, Sarah, Mary Elizabeth ("Betty"). Two other girls, Octavia and Margaret, died of malaria in childhood.

SON: Richard

PETS: Old Whitey (Taylor's warhorse) and a circus pony named Apollo

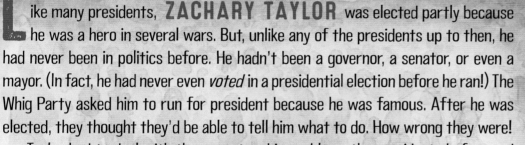

Like many presidents, ZACHARY TAYLOR was elected partly because he was a hero in several wars. But, unlike any of the presidents up to then, he had never been in politics before. He hadn't been a governor, a senator, or even a mayor. (In fact, he had never even *voted* in a presidential election before he ran!) The Whig Party asked him to run for president because he was famous. After he was elected, they thought they'd be able to tell him what to do. How wrong they were!

Taylor had to deal with the same two big problems the presidents before and after him did—new states and slavery. As Americans began to live on land out west, they divided it into territories. As soon as a territory had 60,000 people, it could become a state. That was easy for California, because gold had just been discovered there and people were rushing to get it. But they passed right through territories like New Mexico and Utah, so those territories didn't have many people. Taylor tried to keep it simple: let territories become states whenever they wanted.

Then, when people fought about whether there could be slaves in the new states, his solution was simple again. Even though *he* had slaves, Taylor thought every state should be able to figure it out for itself. One of the big questions was whether you could take your slaves with you if you wanted to move to a free state. Again, Taylor didn't take sides, so *nobody* agreed with him. When Southern leaders threatened to secede if there weren't stronger pro-slavery laws, he countered by saying if they did secede, he would *personally* lead the army against them. But believe it or not, he *himself* bought more slaves while he was president!

In the end, it turned out that Taylor didn't have to decide, because he died just a little over a year after becoming president.

MILLARD FILLMORE

"An honorable defeat is better than a dishonorable victory."

Official portrait by George P. A. Healy

PRESIDENT: July 9, 1850–March 4, 1853

BORN: January 7, 1800

WHERE: Moravia, New York

DIED: March 8, 1874 (age 74)

SISTERS: Olive, Julia, Phoebe

BROTHERS: Almon, Cyrus, Calvin, Darius, Charles

OCCUPATIONS: apprentice clothmaker, lawyer, politician

VICE PRESIDENT: none

PARTY: Whig

WIVES: Abigail Powers Fillmore, Caroline Carmichael Fillmore

DAUGHTER: Mary Abigail ("Abby")

SON: Millard

PETS: two ponies, Mason and Dixon

MILLARD FILLMORE became president when Zachary Taylor died suddenly. Fillmore came from a very poor family, and like many children back then, he couldn't go to school regularly because he had to help work on the farm. But he learned enough on his own to become a lawyer and then spent many years as a member of Congress. That meant he was pretty ready for the job. Though he couldn't settle the fight over slavery, he sure tried. But he found out that sometimes if you try to make everyone happy, everyone ends up angrier than before!

Fillmore tried to make everyone happy by signing a law called the Compromise of 1850. That law gave everybody something, but didn't give anybody *everything*.

What was the compromise? People who were against slavery were happy—at least at first—because California became a state that wouldn't allow slavery. People who were for slavery were happy with the part of the compromise that said owning a slave was just like owning a house or land. This led to what was called the Fugitive Slave Law. It meant that if a slave escaped to a state that didn't allow slavery, the police there still had to arrest him or her. (Yes, women were slaves, too. So were children.) Many police in the North hated slavery and refused to arrest runaway slaves. In fact, some states in the North passed their own laws that said they didn't have to obey this law.

Sometimes compromises do work, but this one didn't. We know that because ten years later, the fight was still going on. By then it had become a war: the Civil War.

YOU CAN LOOK IT UP. Millard Fillmore and his wife Abigail started the first White House library. It had about 200 books. The first ones were a Bible, an atlas, and a dictionary. In fact, Fillmore cared about words so much, he *always* had a dictionary with him. (Nowadays he'd probably carry a smartphone!)

WHAT DOES "D.C." MEAN? The capital of the United States is in Washington, D.C. The "D.C." stands for the District of Columbia. It's a special area that is run differently than a state. That way one state doesn't get to have the capital for the whole country.

A YEARNING FOR LEARNING. Next time your parents see you reading this book, tell them you're an "autodidact," like Millard Fillmore. Then watch the look on their faces! An autodidact is someone who wants to learn so bad, he teaches himself. That's what Millard Fillmore did.

TEACHER'S PET? Millard Fillmore wasn't able to go to school until he was nineteen. His teacher Abigail was only two years older. They stayed in touch after he left school, and they ended up falling in love and getting married six years later.

I am proud to say that **FRANKLIN PIERCE**, the fourteenth president, came from my home state of New Hampshire. But I have to admit he wasn't that special a president.

By now, it must seem like the only thing presidents did back then was to try to get people to agree about slavery! Each time a new state wanted to become part of the United States, the biggest thing people cared about was whether that state would allow slavery or not. That issue kept us from being truly united.

The president and Congress tried to solve the problem in 1820 by using the Mason-Dixon line as a symbolic divider. Free states above, slave states below. But that didn't work. Then they tried the Compromise of 1850, which gave each side something, but neither side everything. By the time Pierce became president just three years later, *that* compromise wasn't working either!

Pierce wanted states to make most of the decisions themselves. He thought that's what the Constitution said. But decisions about slavery in one state made a big difference to people in other states. For example, Pierce thought the United States should buy Cuba from the king of Spain and make it a state. That might have been good for the whole country. But because there were already slaves in Cuba, it would automatically become another slave state. The North didn't like that idea.

Then some congressmen wanted to build the first railroad across the country. That would *definitely* be good for everyone. But the North didn't want it to go through any slave states, and the South didn't like *that* idea.

Leaving the issue of slavery up to each state just didn't work anymore. And Pierce didn't know what to do about it. Like a train coming down the track, the Civil War kept coming closer.

FRANKLIN PIERCE

"The storm of frenzy and faction must inevitably dash itself in vain against the unshaken rock of the Constitution."

PRESIDENTS ARE PEOPLE, TOO. They have the same problems as other people. One of President Pierce's problems was that he drank a *lot* of alcohol. Eventually, he died from a disease caused by heavy drinking.

GET BACK TO SCHOOL! When Pierce was a kid, his parents sent him to a school more than ten miles away. One day he was so homesick, he ran away, making the long journey home on foot. After his parents gave him a nice home-cooked meal, his dad drove him partway back, but then kicked him out of the carriage and made him walk the rest of the way in a thunderstorm!

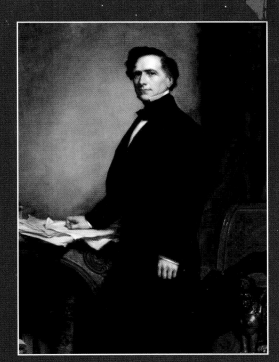

Official portrait by George P. A. Healy

PRESIDENT: March 4, 1853–March 4, 1857

BORN: November 23, 1804

WHERE: Hillsborough, New Hampshire

DIED: October 8, 1869 (age 64)

SISTERS: Nancy, Harriet, and a half sister named Elizabeth. Another sister, Charlotte, died in infancy.

BROTHERS: Benjamin, John, Charles, Henry

OCCUPATIONS: lawyer, soldier, politician

VICE PRESIDENT: William R. King

PARTY: Democratic

NICKNAME: "Young Hickory of the Granite Hills"

WIFE: Jane Appleton Pierce

SONS: Franklin Jr., Franklin, Benjamin. Both Franklins died very young, and Benjamin died in an accident when he was eleven.

PETS: seven little dogs, and two birds that were gifts from Japan!

WHAT A MEMORY! Pierce gave his first speech as president without any notes. It was exactly 3,319 words. That's about ten times as many as are on these two pages.

15 JAMES BUCHANAN

"What is right and what is practicable are two different things."

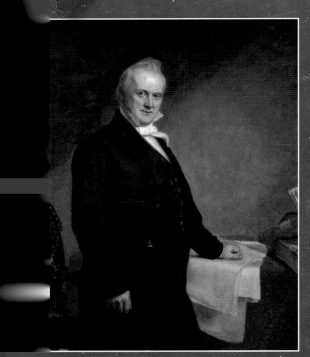

Official portrait by George P. A. Healy

PRESIDENT: March 4, 1857–March 4, 1861

BORN: April 23, 1791

WHERE: Cove Gap, Pennsylvania

DIED: June 1, 1868 (age 77)

SISTERS: Harriet, Sarah, Maria, Elizabeth Jane. Two other sisters, Elizabeth and Mary, died very young.

BROTHERS: Edward, George, William. Another brother, John, died very young.

OCCUPATIONS: lawyer, politician

PARTY: Democratic

VICE PRESIDENT: John C. Breckinridge

NICKNAME: "Old Buck"

WIFE: none. He was the only president never to marry.

WARDS: He cared for two nieces, Mary and Harriet. (Harriet was already in her twenties when her uncle became president, so she was old enough to be the hostess at many White House events—just like a first lady usually does.)

PETS: two dogs—a toy terrier named Punch and a Newfoundland named Laura—and a pair of bald eagles

WHO ARE YOU CALLING A "DOUGHFACE"? That's what some people called Northerners like Buchanan who quietly agreed with slavery. They said people like that twisted their opinions as easily as bread dough to make everyone like them.

IF AT FIRST YOU DON'T SUCCEED . . . Buchanan tried to be president in 1844, 1848, and 1852 before finally being elected in 1856.

WHAT KIND OF PARENT ARE YOU? Buchanan once said that it was against the law for states to leave the Union, but also against the law for the president to stop them. That's like your parents saying you can't play video games, but they can't stop you. (President Buchanan didn't have any kids, so maybe he didn't know any better.)

As the Civil War got closer, disagreements over slavery intensified, and **JAMES BUCHANAN** made them worse.

Even though Buchanan was from the North, he pretty much agreed with the people from the South. Three famous events made that clear.

First, there was the Dred Scott case. A slave whose master had taken him to the North went to the Supreme Court to say he should be free because he was now living in a free state. The judges said no, partly because Buchanan convinced one of them to take his pro-slavery side. (That's something presidents are never supposed to do.)

Next Buchanan tried to force the people of Kansas to allow slavery before they could become a state. The argument ended up in Congress, where there were actually fistfights!

But the most important event of his presidency took place when an abolitionist named John Brown got together a small group of men, including runaway slaves, and attacked a place in Harpers Ferry, Virginia, where the government kept weapons. He lost the battle and was captured and hanged. For many people in the North, he was a hero. People in the South, however, thought his actions would incite a slave rebellion. Historians usually say that the Civil War began when seven states left the United States in 1861. But maybe John Brown *really* fired the first shot two years before.

There was one *good* thing about things getting so *bad*! When it came time to elect a new president in 1860, the country was so divided that neither of the two most famous candidates—Stephen Douglas from Illinois (in the North) and John C. Breckinridge from Kentucky (in the South)—could get enough votes. So the election was won by someone just starting to become well known. . . .

When people ask me who my favorite president is, I usually say **ABRAHAM LINCOLN**. But it's hard to choose just one. However, I *can* say that my favorite presidential quotation is the one on the next page. President Lincoln said it in his first inaugural address. It means he believed that keeping the United States *united* is more important than any one issue. The sentence has words like *mystic* and *angels,* which you might expect to hear in a religious sermon. But Lincoln's words aren't about any particular religion. He is simply saying he has faith that no matter how much we might believe different things, we are still united by the memory of all the people who have died so we could be free.

If you ask people who Lincoln was, most will tell you he's the president who fought the Civil War to free the slaves. The truth is a little more complicated. As soon as he was elected, seven states left the United States to form their own "confederacy" (and four more soon joined them). Their main reason was they wanted to keep slavery legal.

So, yes, Lincoln was against slavery, but for him, fighting the Civil War was just as much about keeping the country together. He succeeded, but at a high cost. Perhaps as many as 750,000 soldiers died—as many as died in all the other wars Americans have fought, *combined.* Yes, that includes World War II and the Vietnam War. Even though the slaves were freed, many African Americans and other minorities are still treated differently and given fewer opportunities to succeed at school and at work. That's called racism. And the Civil War won't *really* be over until we end racism once and for all.

The Civil War ended on April 9, 1865. Five days later, the president was fatally shot.

Lincoln's life is an amazing story. I hope someday you take the time to learn as much about him as you can, because his life and his words tell us so much about what makes this country special.

272 FAMOUS WORDS. Lincoln gave a speech in Gettysburg, Pennsylvania, on November 19, 1863, after the most deadly battle in the Civil War. More than 50,000 soldiers were reported as casualties (dead, wounded, missing, or captured). In just 272 words, he reminded people again that we're *one* United States. Believe it or not, I made a whole film just on that speech. And I've created a website where people recite it, including presidents, movie stars, and other famous people. If you film yourself reciting it, you can be on there, too. Go to learntheaddress.org.

1,754 MORE FAMOUS WORDS. The most important document Lincoln ever *wrote* was the Emancipation Proclamation. *Emancipation* means "freedom." A *proclamation* is an important announcement. It says there should no longer be any slavery in the United States. It wasn't a law yet, but the president wrote it to make his opinion perfectly clear.

A TRAGIC FIRST. Four presidents have been assassinated, but Lincoln was the first. The word *assassination* is often used for murder when a famous person is killed, usually because of what they have said or done. John Wilkes Booth assassinated Lincoln because he was so upset that the president had ended slavery and even wanted to give some African Americans the right to vote.

TRUE FACTS. Lincoln really *was* born in a log cabin with a dirt floor. He really *did* teach himself to be a lawyer, even though he only went to school for one year. And he really *did* keep important papers under his high stovepipe hat.

ABRAHAM LINCOLN

"The mystic chords of memory, stretching from every battlefield and patriot grave to every living heart and hearthstone all over this broad land, will yet swell the chorus of the Union, when again touched, as surely they will be, by the better angels of our nature."

Official portrait by George P. A. Healy

PRESIDENT: March 4, 1861–April 15, 1865

BORN: February 12, 1809

WHERE: Hodgenville, Kentucky

DIED: April 15, 1865 (age 56)

SISTERS: Sarah, and two stepsisters, Elizabeth and Matilda

BROTHER: Thomas, who died in infancy

OCCUPATIONS: postmaster, lawyer, farmer, politician

VICE PRESIDENTS: Hannibal Hamlin, Andrew Johnson

PARTY: Republican

NICKNAME: "Honest Abe"

WIFE: Mary Todd Lincoln

SONS: Robert, who lived to adulthood, and Edward, Willie, and Tad, who all died young

PETS: rabbits; cats; a turkey called Tom; and two goats, Nanny and Nanko

LOOK FOR HIM! $5 bill, 1¢ coin, Lincoln Memorial, Mount Rushmore

WHAT'S AN AMENDMENT? The people who wrote the Constitution couldn't think of everything! But they did think of a really good way to *add* to it if necessary. It's called an amendment. It's not easy to pass one. At least two-thirds of the people in Congress *and* the majority of people in three-quarters of the states have to agree. (Okay, it's a little more complicated, but that's the basic idea.) Sometimes an amendment doesn't just *add* something; it takes an ideal that most Americans hold and makes it more specific—especially when it comes to protecting our freedoms. For example, the Declaration of Independence says, "All men are created equal." But even back then, the Founding Fathers argued about whether "men" meant *all* men (not just white men), and they clearly didn't include women. After the Civil War, the Thirteenth Amendment made it a little clearer by abolishing (ending) slavery. But it took four more years and two more amendments before African American men had *all* the rights of white men. (Yes, it was still men only.)

17 ANDREW JOHNSON

"Slavery exists. It is black in the South, and white in the North."

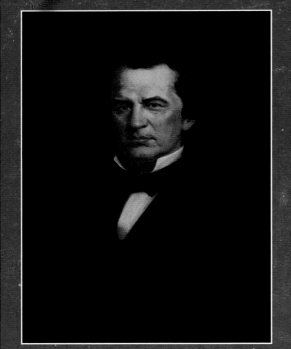

Official portrait by Eliphalet Frazer Andrews

PRESIDENT: April 5, 1865–March 4, 1869

BORN: December 29, 1808

WHERE: Raleigh, North Carolina

DIED: July 31, 1875 (age 66)

BROTHER: William

SISTER: Elizabeth, who died in infancy

OCCUPATIONS: tailor, politician

VICE PRESIDENT: none

PARTY: Democratic

WIFE: Eliza McCardle Johnson

DAUGHTERS: Martha, Mary

SONS: Charles, Robert, Andrew Jr.

PETS: Johnson had no official pets, but left food for a family of white mice who were also living in the White House during his presidency.

After President Lincoln was shot, Vice President ANDREW JOHNSON became president. It was time to "reconstruct" the United States.

Johnson grew up poor in the South, but he stayed in the U.S. Senate during the Civil War. He thought having slaves was okay; he just didn't like the rich people who owned them. And he didn't care if the slaves were freed; he just didn't want them to have the same rights as poor white people. It seems he thought there were simple solutions to all these problems.

Unfortunately, there weren't simple solutions . . . and there were a *lot* of problems. Should the freed slaves be allowed to vote? Where would they live? How could they get jobs? What did the Southern states have to do to rejoin the Union? Should their leaders go to jail?

Just because you won a war doesn't mean you can do whatever you want. Just because you lost doesn't mean you have to do everything the winner says. The North wanted to make things as easy as possible for the former slaves. The South wanted to make things as difficult as possible. Every time Congress passed a law to help freed slaves, the Southern states would pass laws to make it harder for them.

To complicate things even more, Johnson thought the congressmen from the North were trying to go too fast. So when they tried passing laws that gave more rights to the freed slaves, he kept vetoing them. Some Northern congressmen were so frustrated they impeached Johnson—something that had never happened before. To *impeach* someone is like accusing them of a crime. The next step is to have a trial in the Senate. When Johnson was tried, he was found not guilty by just one vote. Seven months later, he was out of office anyway because he lost the election of 1868. That's when the real work of postwar reconstruction began.

TWO VERY DIFFERENT PRESIDENT JOHNSONS. In 1866, Andrew Johnson *vetoed* a law called the Civil Rights Act, which tried to define what it meant to be a citizen of the United States. Nearly one hundred years later (in 1964), President Lyndon Johnson (no relation) *signed* a Civil Rights Act. Believe it or not, both laws were still trying to explain what Thomas Jefferson meant when he said that all men are created equal.

PRESIDENT TAILOR? When Andrew Johnson took office, there had already been a President Taylor. But Johnson was the first president *tailor.* He had learned to make clothes as a kid to help support his family. He only wore suits he had made himself.

"**STATES' RIGHTS.**" Think about this for a second: Congress passes laws. The states pass laws. What if Congress passes a law that's different from a state law? That happened a *lot* before and after the Civil War. Many people in the South felt that—even though the slaves were free—their state government could still pass laws to keep these former slaves from having the same rights as white people. Today you probably hear people having similar arguments over different issues, like who can get married or who can become a citizen—issues society can't agree on. Who should decide? The states or the country?

13 + 14 + 15 = 1? The Thirteenth Amendment ended slavery. You might think that would give former slaves the same rights as everyone else. But plenty of people *didn't* think so. It took the Fourteenth Amendment to make those former slaves real citizens, and the Fifteenth to say they were allowed to vote. (Women had to wait for the Nineteenth for that right.)

WAKE UP! My friend the author and historian Shelby Foote said that Grant had "four o'clock in the morning courage." That meant if his soldiers woke him up at 4 a.m. to deal with a crisis, he could get up right away, stay calm, focus, and make good decisions.

WHO WAS ULYSSES? Grant's parents originally named him Hiram Ulysses Grant. Later, when he went to West Point, he was mistakenly registered with the initials U.S. Grant. He liked it, so he kept it. Ulysses may sound like a strange name, but it is the name of one of the most heroic warriors in ancient myths. Like Grant, he was able to think of very clever ways to win battles. When it came to naming Grant, his parents made the perfect choice.

SMILE! When the famous writer Mark Twain met Grant, he said the president looked like a man "who had not smiled for seven years, and who was not intending to smile for another seven." But they soon became good friends. In fact, Twain published Grant's memoirs.

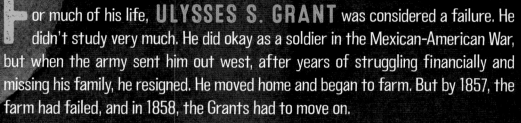

"I have never advocated war except as a means of peace."

For much of his life, **ULYSSES S. GRANT** was considered a failure. He didn't study very much. He did okay as a soldier in the Mexican-American War, but when the army sent him out west, after years of struggling financially and missing his family, he resigned. He moved home and began to farm. But by 1857, the farm had failed, and in 1858, the Grants had to move on.

So it's kind of amazing that by 1864, this "failure" was leading the entire Union Army. And in 1868, he was elected president of the United States.

What changed? Maybe nothing. Maybe all those failures taught him how to have courage and keep going, even in the face of difficulties. During the Civil War, he led his soldiers again and again into dangerous battles. Other generals thought he was too reckless. But President Lincoln said, "I can't spare this man—he fights."

When Grant was asked to run for president, he told people he knew nothing of politics. However, just as he had fought hard to free the slaves, as president he fought hard to make sure they were treated as equals. He encouraged other countries to free their slaves, too.

A lot of people think Grant was a better general than president because he gave some important jobs to corrupt people, and they did things that made many Americans lose confidence in their government. When Grant was done being president, he apologized for his "errors of judgment."

Toward the end of his life, Grant was back where he started. He had lost all his money in a bad business deal. He was also dying of throat cancer. But he decided to write his memoirs so his family would have money to live on. Even though he was in great pain, he still had courage. He still kept going. He finished his book a few days before he died.

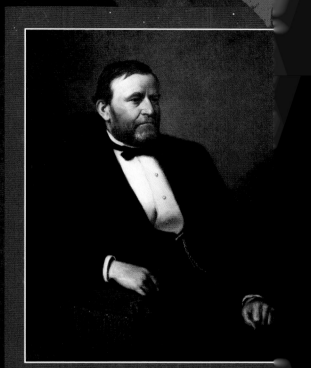

Official portrait by Henry Ulke

PRESIDENT: March 4, 1869–March 4, 1877
BORN: April 27, 1822
WHERE: Point Pleasant, Ohio
DIED: July 23, 1885 (age 63)
SISTERS: Clara, Virginia ("Jennie"), Mary
BROTHERS: Samuel, Orvil
OCCUPATIONS: soldier, farmer, shopkeeper, U.S. Army general
VICE PRESIDENTS: Schuyler Colfax, Henry Wilson
PARTY: Republican
NICKNAME: "Hero of Appomattox"
WIFE: Julia Dent Grant
DAUGHTER: Ellen ("Nellie")
SONS: Frederick, Ulysses Jr. ("Buck"), Jesse
PETS: numerous horses, including his warhorse Jeff Davis, his saddle horse Cincinnatus, ponies, carriage horses, and racing horses; and Rosie the dog
LOOK FOR HIM! $50 bill, Grant's Tomb

UNCONDITIONAL. After winning one of the Union's first major victories in the Civil War, Grant declared that "no terms except an unconditional and immediate surrender can be accepted," leading many to call him "Unconditional Surrender" Grant. But Grant wasn't always unconditional. When he accepted the surrender of General Robert E. Lee's Confederate forces in April 1865, he agreed to allow the soldiers to retain their weapons and horses and return to their homes—a very gracious deal.

RUTHERFORD B. HAYES

"He serves his party best who serves his country best."

Official portrait by Daniel Huntington

PRESIDENT: March 4, 1877–March 4, 1881

BORN: October 4, 1822

WHERE: Delaware, Ohio

DIED: January 17, 1893 (age 70)

SISTERS: Fanny. Another sister, Sarah, died in early childhood.

BROTHER: Lorenzo. He drowned when Rutherford was only two years old.

OCCUPATIONS: lawyer, soldier, politician

VICE PRESIDENT: William A. Wheeler

PARTY: Republican

WIFE: Lucy Ware Webb Hayes

DAUGHTER: Fanny

SONS: Birchard, James, Rutherford, Scott. Three other sons—Joseph, George, and Manning—died very young.

PETS: a Siamese cat named Siam; dogs named Grim, Duke, Hector, and Dot; and cows, horses, goats, and canaries!

RUTHERFORD B. HAYES became president in 1877, even though he received almost 300,000 *fewer* votes than his rival, Samuel J. Tilden. The reason people didn't agree that Tilden was the winner is that both sides said the other one had cheated, especially in certain states. When representatives from all the states came together (in the Electoral College), *they* couldn't agree on a winner either. Finally, Congress had to decide. They elected Hayes by just one vote.

Before becoming president, Hayes went to Harvard Law School and was a lawyer until he joined the Union Army. In the Civil War, he had four horses shot out from under him! He was nominated for Congress during the war but refused to come home to fight to be elected, because he felt it was more important to fight for his country. He still won. Later he served as the governor of Ohio for nine years.

President Hayes worked hard to bring people together after the Civil War. He wanted to protect the rights of the newly freed slaves. He even consulted with Frederick Douglass, the renowned African American statesman and reformer. He also wanted to protect the rights of Native Americans. But he didn't stop states and towns from passing "Jim Crow" laws, which took away rights instead. Many of those laws lasted for almost a hundred years.

His wife, Lucy, was the *first* first lady to have gone to college. In 1850, she graduated from Wesleyan Women's College, which is now part of Ohio Wesleyan University. She was very much against slavery and was an important adviser to President Hayes.

President Hayes promised to serve just one term, and that's what he did. But after he left office, he continued to try to help veterans and encourage governments to make education available for everyone.

AN EASTER TRADITION. Rutherford B. Hayes's wife, Lucy, began the popular White House Easter Egg Roll, a race in which kids roll hard-boiled eggs down the lawn with long-handled spoons. Last one to finish is a rotten egg!

AGITATE . . . AGITATE . . . AGITATE. That's the advice the great African American statesman Frederick Douglass gave a young man who wanted to know what to do with his life. Douglass, along with Harriet Tubman and Sojourner Truth, led the fight to get *real* equal rights for African Americans after the Civil War. All three of them had escaped slavery (or, as Douglass put it, stole themselves away from their masters) and wanted to end discrimination once and for all. One time Douglass went to the White House to try to convince President Hayes to stop states from passing laws that treated African Americans like "second-class citizens." He didn't succeed, but they kept on "agitating." Change came, but slowly . . . there were still laws like that in some states for almost another one hundred years.

GIVE ME A CALL. Alexander Graham Bell, the famous inventor, installed the first telephone in the White House for Rutherford B. Hayes. The president's first telephone call was between him and Bell, who was waiting thirteen miles away. Supposedly, Hayes's first words were "Please speak more slowly."

It's sad to say, but President **JAMES A. GARFIELD** is best known for being assassinated. Just ten months after being elected, he was shot in the back by a man who was angry (and some say driven insane) because he had supported Garfield's campaign but wasn't offered a job in the new government.

You could say that Garfield was actually killed by his doctors. Back then, a British doctor named Joseph Lister was telling surgeons it was important to use "antiseptics" to kill germs on their hands and tools before operating, in order to prevent infections. (Listerine mouthwash is named for him.) However, many doctors didn't believe him. During surgery, they'd drop their tools on the floor and just pick them up and keep using them. They didn't even wash their hands. When Garfield died two and a half months after being shot, it wasn't from the bullet. It was from infections caused by the doctors. Today he would have lived.

Even though his family was very poor and his father died when Garfield was only two, his mother worked hard so he could get an education. She even managed to save enough to send him to college, where he worked as a janitor to keep paying for his classes. But that's where he found out he really loved learning. After he graduated, he became a professor. He was an abolitionist—someone who was strongly against slavery—so when the Civil War came, he volunteered and soon became a general. After the war, he was in Congress for almost twenty years before becoming president.

President Garfield did have time to begin work on several important projects as president. He is best known for trying to stop political "patronage." That means giving people jobs in government because they're friends or they gave you money to get re-elected. Garfield was the first president who really made people aware of how big a problem it was.

JAMES A. GARFIELD

"Ideas are the great warriors of the world."

TWO HANDS ARE BETTER THAN ONE. President Garfield was a lefty. But he could actually write with both hands at once . . . in two different languages (French and German)! Plus, he kept a diary in Latin.

MAN OVERBOARD! My favorite story about Garfield is that when he was sixteen, he went to work on a boat and fell overboard fourteen times in just six weeks! He was probably better off going to college.

WHAT DID HE HAVE TO LOSE? State legislatures used to elect their U.S. senators (instead of having the people vote for them). On January 6, 1880, the Ohio legislature chose James Garfield. Later in the year, the Republican Party nominated him to run for president (which surprised him and just about everybody else). But what did he have to lose? Even if he lost the presidential election, he would still have been a senator!

SPEAKING THEIR LANGUAGE. Since people come to America from all over the world, English is often their second language. Voters like it when someone running for president tries to say at least a few words in their native language. Garfield was the first person to do that—he gave speeches in German, as well as English.

Official portrait by Calvin Curtis

PRESIDENT: March 4, 1881–September 19, 1881

BORN: November 19, 1831

WHERE: Moreland Hills, Ohio

DIED: September 19, 1881 (age 49)

SISTERS: Mary, Mehitable

BROTHERS: Thomas. Another brother, James, died as a young child.

OCCUPATIONS: lawyer, teacher, preacher, janitor, carpenter, soldier, U.S. Army general, politician

VICE PRESIDENT: Chester A. Arthur

PARTY: Republican

WIFE: Lucretia Rudolph Garfield

DAUGHTERS: Mary ("Mollie"). Another daughter, Eliza, died very young.

SONS: Harry ("Hal"), James, Irvin, Abram. Another son, Edward ("Ned"), died very young.

PETS: Veto, a Newfoundland dog; and Kit, Mollie's mare

CHESTER A. ARTHUR

"Good ballplayers make good citizens."

LIVING DANGEROUSLY . . . Chester Arthur became president when President Garfield was assassinated. But Congress still didn't put anyone special in charge of protecting the president. I guess Arthur wasn't too worried about it. He'd stay up way after midnight and walk around Washington with his friends. That would never happen today unless the president went out with a *lot* of people from the Secret Service.

ONE LEG AT A TIME! President Arthur was called "Elegant Arthur" because he was a fancy dresser. He had more than eighty pairs of pants and changed them several times a day!

Official portrait by Daniel Huntington

PRESIDENT: September 19, 1881–March 4, 1885

BORN: October 5, 1829

WHERE: Fairfield, Vermont

DIED: November 18, 1886 (age 57)

SISTERS: Regina, Jane, Almeda, Ann Eliza, Malvina, Mary

BROTHERS: William. Another brother, George, died in childhood.

OCCUPATIONS: teacher, lawyer, tax collector, politician

VICE PRESIDENT: none

PARTY: Republican

NICKNAME: "Elegant Arthur"

WIFE: Ellen Lewis Herndon Arthur

DAUGHTER: Ellen ("Nell")

SONS: Chester II. Another son, William, died very young.

PETS: horses

Becoming president can change people. **CHESTER A. ARTHUR** is a good example. Before he was elected, people thought he wasn't very honest. For many years, he had worked with a senator from New York with the wonderful name of Roscoe Conkling! Roscoe and his buddies would force people to pay money (a practice known as "graft") if they wanted to get things done. For example, Conkling got Arthur the job of collecting taxes from ships that arrived in New York Harbor. If captains wanted to unload their cargo, they had to pay up first. Many people think Arthur charged a little extra so some sailors would be allowed to unload their goods before others . . . and that he kept that little extra for himself.

Chester Arthur had never been elected to *anything* before becoming vice president. So when he became president, people expected him to continue his "corrupt" ways. Instead, he helped to pass laws that stopped people from giving government jobs to their best friends. Everyone who applied had to pass a test. They still do. It's called the civil service exam. He also vetoed a law that paid for big projects like roads and bridges and canals because he was afraid there was too much "extra" money requested to do the job.

President Arthur also made the U.S. Navy much stronger and tried to protect the rights of minorities—particularly ex-slaves and the many new immigrants from China. A lot of people thought Chester Arthur would be a weak president who would do whatever other people told him to do. But he ended up having his own ideas about what was best for America, and was often able to get Congress to go along. That's what I meant when I said at the beginning that becoming president can change people.

WE VOTED FOR CHESTER! While I was writing this book, our family got a new puppy. I wanted to name him something presidential, and my wife liked the name Chester, so it was an easy choice for us. Our daughters, however, wanted us to call him "Marshmallow," which isn't very presidential. The compromise? Chester Marshmallow Burns!

HEY, WHERE WERE YOU BORN? The Constitution says you have to be a U.S. citizen to be president. Does that mean you have to be born in America? Or that your parents are citizens? Arthur's father didn't become a citizen until *after* Chester was born. His mom *was* a citizen but moved to Canada and back again *before* he was born. Some people claimed *he* was actually born in Canada instead of northern Vermont. That's not true. In the same way, some people tried to say President Obama was born in Africa instead of Hawaii. *That's* not true either.

43

"PICK UP THE PHONE!" When the phone rang at the White House, President Cleveland answered it himself. (Today there are fourteen operators answering 4,000 calls a day.)

WELCOME TO AMERICA! On October 28, 1886, Grover Cleveland dedicated the Statue of Liberty in New York Harbor. It's become a powerful symbol of freedom, especially for the millions of immigrants who see it when they first arrive in America. On a plaque inside the base, there's a poem that includes these famous words: "Give me your tired, your poor, your huddled masses yearning to breathe free."

CHECKS AND BALANCES. Even though this book is about presidents, they represent just one of the three branches of government. The other two are the Congress and the Supreme Court. For a law to become official, Congress (both the House *and* the Senate) has to pass it and the president has to sign it. If some people think that the law goes against what the Constitution says is right, they can ask the Supreme Court to decide. We call that checks and balances. In other words, each branch of government can *check* what the other is doing, which helps to strike a *balance* between different points of view.

THE POKER-PLAYING PRESIDENT. Cleveland didn't care about the fancy food and formal events at the White House. He was happier fishing, hunting, drinking, and playing poker with his friends.

Official portrait by Eastman Johnson

PRESIDENT: March 4, 1885–March 4, 1889

BORN: March 18, 1837

WHERE: Caldwell, New Jersey

DIED: June 24, 1908 (age 71)

SISTERS: Ann, Mary, Margaret, Susan, Rose

BROTHERS: William, Richard, Lewis

OCCUPATIONS: sheriff, lawyer, politician

VICE PRESIDENT: Thomas Hendricks (in his first term)

PARTY: Democratic

NICKNAMES: "Veto President," "President Who Said 'No!'"

WIFE: Frances Folsom Cleveland

DAUGHTERS: ("Baby") Ruth, Esther, Marion

SONS: Richard ("Dick"), Francis, Oscar (Oscar was born to a mother who didn't have a husband. Grover Cleveland helped support him and his mother, though we don't know who Oscar's father was.)

PETS: dogs of many breeds, including a cocker spaniel, a collie, a Saint Bernard, dachshunds, foxhounds, and a French poodle called Hector. Also ponies, birds, game chickens, and hundreds of fish!

LOOK FOR HIM . . . OR NOT! Grover Cleveland is on the $1,000 bill, though it is now out of circulation.

GROVER CLEVELAND was once called a "good man in a bad trade." He always tried to tell the truth and do what he believed was right. But some politicians aren't always honest and will even do things they know are wrong just to get elected—or to make a little extra money. As governor of New York, Cleveland tried to stop this kind of corruption. That's one reason he was elected president.

People—and presidents—have different beliefs about what's right. We've seen presidents who believed states should make most of the rules, and others who believed the federal government should; presidents who wanted equal rights for freed slaves, and others who believed it was okay to treat them as second-class citizens. Soon we'll be talking about presidents with *very* different beliefs about the right way to treat other countries.

People in Congress have different beliefs, too. So if a president really wants to get things done, he often has to compromise. Grover Cleveland was not very good at compromising. He was even called the President Who Said "No!" because he vetoed 414 bills.

One reason he said no so often is that he believed the federal government could *only* do what the Constitution said it could do. But things were starting to happen that the Founding Fathers couldn't have predicted. In particular, as the country got bigger, the farmers, bankers, and businesses in different states were beginning to depend on one another more. Grover Cleveland believed it was up to the states to keep things fair. But sometimes only the federal government can make sure that everyone is playing by the same rules.

BENJAMIN HARRISON

"We Americans have no commission from God to police the world."

Official portrait by Eastman Johnson

PRESIDENT: March 4, 1889–March 4, 1893

BORN: August 20, 1833

WHERE: North Bend, Ohio

DIED: March 13, 1901 (age 67)

SISTERS: Mary. Another sister, Anna, died in childhood.

BROTHERS: Archibald, Carter, John Scott. Four brothers—William, John, James, and James—died in childhood.

OCCUPATIONS: lawyer, soldier, journalist, politician

VICE PRESIDENT: Levi P. Morton

PARTY: Republican

NICKNAMES: "Kid Gloves Harrison," "Human Iceberg"

WIVES: Caroline Scott Harrison, Mary Scott Lord Dimmick Harrison

DAUGHTERS: Mary ("Mamie"), Elizabeth (from his second marriage). Another daughter died in infancy.

SON: Russell

PETS: opossums named Mr. Reciprocity and Mr. Protection; dogs; and a billy goat named Old Whiskers, whom President Harrison personally chased through Washington, D.C., after he got away from the White House

BENJAMIN HARRISON isn't very well known. In fact, people often get him confused with the ninth president—his grandfather William Henry Harrison. Of course, the elder Harrison was only in office for a month. Benjamin Harrison served a full term, and actually a lot happened during those four years.

We sometimes think that certain presidents were more on the side of rich people than poor people, or were on the side of people in the North more than those in the South. It's usually not that simple.

For example, President Harrison signed a law called the Sherman Anti-Trust Act that kept big companies from making secret agreements to keep prices high. But he also signed a tariff bill that was good for business and raised a lot of money for the government. The government used that money to help old Civil War (Union) soldiers from the *North*, but didn't do anything for old Confederate soldiers in the *South*.

Then Harrison signed a bill called the Sherman Silver Purchase Act that was great for states in the *West*, where there was a lot of silver, but not so good for bankers and big businesses in the *East*.

That's one of the hardest things about being president. Everything you do will probably help some people but make life more difficult for others. It's easy to forget we are one *United* States.

Do you wonder why those laws were called "Sherman" acts instead of "Harrison" acts? They are named for John Sherman, a lawyer from Ohio who was in Congress for thirty-eight years. He tried to become president three times but failed. Still, he wrote some of the most important laws in American history. He proved you don't have to *be* president to be as important as someone who *is* president.

THE "COLDEST" PRESIDENT? Benjamin Harrison just wasn't that much fun to be with. He thought the president should *always* act formal and dignified instead of like a regular guy. In fact, one of his nicknames was the "Human Iceberg."

YOU'RE WELCOME! An "immigration station" is the first stop for people who have come from other countries to live here. The famous one on Ellis Island, in New York Harbor near the Statue of Liberty, opened on January 1, 1892. Over the next sixty years, more than 12 million people passed through Ellis Island.

IN '88, AS THEY DID THEN—
We roll it now for gallant BEN.

The spirit of our men is up.
...cky hills to ocean.

AMERI...
IN ...

FREE TRADE notion,
Country in commotion.

THE R...
WHAT...

OLD ALLEGANY IN 1840
started the BALL for HARRISON

TARIFFS. Tariffs are taxes we charge companies in other countries to sell their products over here. For example, say you own a company in America that makes fancy sweatshirts with your favorite team's logo on them, and there's a company in another country that makes them cheaper. If the government puts a tariff on clothes from that other country, their sweatshirts will cost as much as yours. However, prices will go up for everyone. States argue about tariffs all the time because they are usually good for people in some states and bad for others.

47

GROVER CLEVELAND did something no other president has ever done. He won a presidential election (1884), then he lost one (1888), and then he won again (1892). In the election of 1888, more *people* voted for Grover Cleveland, but more *state* votes went to Benjamin Harrison . . . so he won! That is one of the most confusing things in American politics. You could say Grover Cleveland had the "last laugh," however, because in 1892 he won the "people" *and* the "state" votes and became "Grover Cleveland, again!"

By his second term, the country was growing faster than ever. It seemed like anything that happened in one place affected people everywhere else. For example, factories in the eastern United States were making everything from clothes to carriages. But they needed to hire more people to keep growing. In the South and West, there were more families starting farms. But it cost a lot of money to buy the equipment they needed. So both the factory owners and the farmers needed to borrow money from banks to run their businesses. And in order to have enough money to lend, banks needed people to put their money in them. That meant people who put their money in those banks had to trust the banks to keep it safe.

In the late 1880s and early 1890s, there wasn't enough rain, and that caused severe droughts. By the time Cleveland became president again, many farmers didn't have enough food to sell (or sometimes even to feed their own families). When they couldn't pay the banks back, they lost their land, so they stopped buying supplies and equipment. Pretty soon, farmers were starving, factories were closing, and workers were losing their jobs. People became nervous and took their savings out of the banks. This was called the Panic of 1893.

What did Grover Cleveland do about it? Unfortunately, as far as most farmers and workers were concerned, not enough. He still believed that he and Congress could do only what the Constitution said they could do. However, America was changing, and it was time for the government to start changing, too.

ELECTORAL VOTES VS. POPULAR VOTES. In some presidential elections, the person with the most votes actually *loses*. Strange, huh? That's because the winner is chosen based on the number of state ("electoral") votes rather than the number of people ("popular") votes, and big states have more votes than little states because they have more people. If you want to learn more, find a map of the Electoral College that shows how many votes each state has today.

ANOTHER REASON NOT TO SMOKE. In 1893, Cleveland got cancer in his mouth from smoking a pipe. He had doctors remove the cancer secretly so people wouldn't get scared that the president might die. Fortunately, his mustache covered up the results of the surgery.

GROVER CLEVELAND, AGAIN!

"What is the use of being elected or re-elected unless you stand for something?"

Official portrait by Eastman Johnson

PRESIDENT: March 4, 1893–March 4, 1897

VICE PRESIDENT: Adlai Stevenson I (in his second term)

PARTY: Democratic

GROVER CLEVELAND, *AGAIN?*

When my kids were growing up, they liked to memorize the names of the presidents. Every time they got to Grover Cleveland's second term as president, we'd all shout, "Grover Cleveland, again!" (That's where I got the title of this book.)

Do *you* want to try?

George _____	Abraham _____	Herbert _____
John _____	Andrew _____	Franklin _____
Thomas _____	Ulysses _____	Harry _____
James _____	Rutherford _____	Dwight _____
James _____	James _____	John _____
John _____	Chester _____	Lyndon _____
Andrew _____	Grover _____	Richard _____
Martin _____	Benjamin _____	Gerald _____
William _____	Grover _____	Jimmy _____
John _____	William _____	Ronald _____
James _____	Theodore _____	George _____
Zachary _____	William _____	Bill _____
Millard _____	Woodrow _____	George _____
Franklin _____	Warren _____	Barack _____
James _____	Calvin _____	

"I DO!" Cleveland was the only president to get married in the White House. He was forty-eight. His wife, Frances, was just twenty-one—the youngest first lady ever. When her husband lost the presidency in 1884, Frances told people who worked at the White House, "We'll be back!" Nobody believed her. But she was right.

"War should never be entered upon until every agency of peace has failed."

Official portrait by Harriet Anderson Stubbs Murphy

PRESIDENT: March 4, 1897–September 14, 1901

BORN: January 29, 1843

WHERE: Niles, Ohio

DIED: September 14, 1901 (age 58)

SISTERS: Anna ("Annie"), Mary, Helen, Sarah. Abigail ("Abbie") died in infancy.

BROTHERS: David, James, Abner

OCCUPATIONS: soldier, lawyer, politician

VICE PRESIDENTS: Garret Hobart, Theodore Roosevelt

PARTY: Republican

NICKNAME: "Idol of Ohio"

WIFE: Ida Saxton McKinley

DAUGHTERS: Two daughters, Katherine ("Katie") and Ida, died very young.

PETS: a Mexican yellow-headed parrot named Washington Post, two Angora kittens named Valeriano Weyler and Enrique DeLome, and roosters

LOOK FOR HIM . . . OR NOT! on the $500 bill (though no longer in circulation). The highest point in North America used to be named for him (Mount McKinley in Alaska), but President Obama changed the official name to Denali in 2015, which is what the native Alaskans called it all along.

MONEY. What *is* money, anyway? Why do stores give you food and clothes and video games just because you or your parents give them some pieces of paper or a plastic card? Really smart people spend their whole lives trying to understand this, so don't worry if you don't know the answer. All I know is that money isn't worth anything unless we *trust* each other, the banks, and the government.

OFF TO SEE THE WIZARD? Here's a really strange one: some people say that L. Frank Baum based his book *The Wizard of Oz* on what was actually happening in the United States at the time. For example, gold comes in yellow bricks, so the yellow brick road is actually about using just gold for government money. Dorothy had silver slippers, so she must have preferred silver. (In the movie version, the filmmakers gave her ruby slippers, probably to show off how neat films in color could be.) The Wizard, they say, was McKinley, and the Emerald City was Washington, D.C.

ntil **WILLIAM McKINLEY** won the election in 1896, presidents spent most of their time trying to solve problems in America. McKinley spent just as much time trying to solve problems in other countries.

For centuries, Cuba, the Philippines, Puerto Rico, and other nations had belonged to Spain (just like we had once belonged to England). Now they wanted to be free—particularly the people in Cuba, who had been fighting for independence for many years. We went to war to help them and ended up defeating the Spanish there and in other countries, too. The entire war took just ten weeks! So those countries became independent. Sort of. Some people in those countries wanted us to protect them. Some others thought we wanted to boss them around.

Here in America, President McKinley faced the same question presidents *always* have to think about: what can the country do to help people have a safe place to live and food to eat? The answer depends partly on how much money the government has. Back then, everyone thought *that* depended on how much gold the government had. Other people thought it should also depend on how much silver we had.

The gold way usually helped rich people. The gold *and* silver way usually helped ordinary people—because it could make things cost less. McKinley was pretty much on the gold side. Historians think that might be one reason why, less than a year after McKinley was re-elected in 1900, a man named Leon Czolgosz assassinated him. Czolgosz blamed McKinley for the fact that rich people kept getting richer and poor people kept getting poorer. He believed that this kind of "social injustice" wasn't fair and that it was the government's fault.

When McKinley died, the vice president took over. Theodore Roosevelt was the most famous soldier of the war with Spain and would become one of the most famous presidents in American history.

IT'S NOT WHETHER YOU WIN OR LOSE. The man who ran for president against William McKinley was almost as famous as he was. His name was William Jennings Bryan and he was the youngest person to ever run for president. He tried three times and never won, but he did a lot to make people aware of how hard life could be for farmers and ordinary workers.

SECRET SERVICE. Before the 1900s, there weren't any people who were specially trained to protect presidents. After President McKinley was shot, however, Congress was determined that it never happen again. So they voted to have special agents in the Secret Service, whose usual duty was to catch counterfeiters, protect presidents at all times. Only one president has been killed since.

It takes a lot of energy to be president. THEODORE ROOSEVELT had enough energy for ten presidents! He hiked in the wilderness and swam in icy rivers. He rode horses for hours at a time, went exploring and hunting, read two or three books a day, and wrote more than thirty-five books and about 150,000 letters.

Elected vice president in 1896, Roosevelt became president when William McKinley was assassinated. Until then, he was best known for leading a band of soldiers called the Rough Riders during the Spanish-American War. Now he was about to lead the entire country into the twentieth century.

Nearly eighty years before Roosevelt became president, James Monroe said that we would protect any country in North or South America from being taken over by any country in Europe. Theodore Roosevelt took that idea one step further. He said that if the leaders of any country in the Americas weren't treating their people well, we could help put other leaders in their place. That's not always such a good idea. Can you imagine another country deciding who should be *our* president? Sometimes America has used that as an excuse to get something *we* want. Have you heard of the Panama Canal, which gives boats a shortcut from the Atlantic Ocean to the Pacific? In order to make it happen, Roosevelt promoted a revolution in Panama, which was then a province of Colombia, because we—and many Panamanians—wanted that canal built. Panama became a separate country, where we had a lot of influence.

Here in America, Roosevelt had a big plan called the Square Deal. He wanted to make sure that food and drugs were safer, that the places where people worked were less dangerous, and that companies charged fair prices.

Roosevelt has been called the "Conservationist President" because he created the U.S. Forest Service. He also added land to the National Park System. By doing these things, he kept millions of acres wild, so no one can build there (and we can take trips there!).

I know that sounds like a lot . . . but that was just a little of what Theodore Roosevelt did. By the way, his favorite expression was "Bully!" To him, it didn't mean someone who pushed you around; it meant "Remarkable!" or "Awesome!" He was definitely one of our most remarkable presidents.

YOU CAN'T STOP ME! Since Roosevelt had served most of President McKinley's term *and* one of his own, he decided not to run again in 1908. But by 1912, he had changed his mind. One evening during the 1912 campaign, he was giving a speech in Milwaukee, Wisconsin, and a man just seven feet away shot him in the chest. Fortunately, the bullet was slowed down by the fifty-page speech and eyeglass case in his pocket. He was bleeding badly, but *that* couldn't stop him. He continued speaking for almost an hour and a half!

PONY EXPRESS? Roosevelt's children loved playing pranks. Once they even brought a pony into the White House and gave it a ride in the elevator.

THEODORE ROOSEVELT

"I have always been fond of the West African proverb 'Speak softly and carry a big stick; you will go far.'"

Official portrait by John Singer Sargent

PRESIDENT: September 14, 1901–March 4, 1909

BORN: October 27, 1858

WHERE: New York, New York

DIED: January 6, 1919 (age 60)

SISTERS: Anna ("Bamie"), Corinne

BROTHER: Elliott

OCCUPATIONS: rancher, soldier, politician

VICE PRESIDENTS: none in his first term, Charles Fairbanks (in his second term)

PARTY: Republican

NICKNAMES: "TR," "Teddy"

WIVES: Alice Lee Roosevelt, Edith Carow Roosevelt

DAUGHTERS: Alice ("Princess Alice"), from his first marriage, and Ethel

SONS: Theodore Jr. ("Ted"), Kermit, Archibald ("Archie"), Quentin

PETS: a menagerie of animals that included horses and ponies, dogs, cats, birds, five bears, a badger, a flying squirrel, a lion, a hyena, a zebra, a raccoon, a pig, and Alice's pet snake, Emily Spinach

LOOK FOR HIM! Mount Rushmore

SADDEST DAY OF HIS LIFE. On Valentine's Day 1884, when Theodore Roosevelt was just twenty-five years old, his mother and his wife both died within hours of each other in the same house. He was so depressed he went out west to work at a ranch and go horseback riding. He called depression "the black care," and said that the "black care rarely sits behind a rider whose pace is fast enough."

27 WILLIAM HOWARD TAFT

"We are all imperfect. We cannot expect perfect government."

Official portrait by Anders Zorn

PRESIDENT: March 4, 1909–March 4, 1913

BORN: September 15, 1857

WHERE: Cincinnati, Ohio

DIED: March 8, 1930 (age 72)

SISTER: Frances ("Fanny")

BROTHERS: Henry, Horace, and Samuel (who died in infancy), as well as two half brothers, Charles and Peter ("Rossy")

OCCUPATIONS: lawyer, judge, law school dean, politician, chief justice of the Supreme Court

VICE PRESIDENT: James Sherman

PARTY: Republican

WIFE: Helen ("Nellie") Herron Taft

DAUGHTER: Helen

SONS: Robert, Charles

PETS: a dog named Caruso; and the last cows at the White House, Pauline Wayne (Taft loved her fresh milk) and Mooly Wooly

BATTER UP! In 1910, Taft became the first president to throw out the ball on Opening Day of the baseball season. (The game was between the Washington Senators and the Brooklyn Dodgers.)

RUB-A-DUB . . . Taft was so big, they say that the first time he tried to take a bath in the White House he got stuck! A special oversized tub had to be put in the bathroom for him.

"TWO OUT OF THREE AIN'T BAD." Back when we were talking about Grover Cleveland (as opposed to Grover Cleveland, again!), I explained the three branches of government: the executive, headed by the president; the legislative, represented by Congress; and the judicial, represented by the Supreme Court. William Howard Taft is the only person who was ever the president *and* chief justice of the Supreme Court. (But not at the same time.)

Shortly after Theodore Roosevelt was elected in 1904, he told people he wouldn't run for president again. He regretted saying it almost right away, and by the election of 1908, he *really* regretted it. So he did the next-best thing. He told the Republican Party to nominate one of his closest friends, Secretary of War **WILLIAM HOWARD TAFT**, because Taft had always seemed willing to do just about whatever TR wanted. Like all presidents, once Taft took office, he started doing things *his* way. Whereas Roosevelt was well known as a progressive who loved trying new things, Taft was a little more conservative.

However, as we've seen, presidents are never completely on one side or the other. Taft spent much of his term trying to balance conservative and progressive principles. For example, he signed a law that made sure the rates for railroad tickets and telephones stayed fair. He even supported the idea that businesses should pay taxes. No president had ever been in favor of that before.

TR thought Taft cared more about how other countries treated *our* businesses than how they protected *their* people's freedom, so he was particularly upset that Taft didn't do something about the fact we weren't protecting Chinese immigrants' freedom. Many of the immigrants who had left China in search of a better life in America were interrogated, detained, and deported from Angel Island, an infamous immigration station near San Francisco. That meant they were being excluded and told they weren't welcome in America! Taft also tried to take some of the land that Roosevelt had made part of the National Park System so businesses could mine coal there. That made TR *really* mad. By 1912, TR was so mad he decided to run for president again! (Who did he think he was . . . Grover Cleveland?)

One of the most famous things about William Howard Taft is one of the least important: he weighed 332 pounds, more than any other president. That brings me to one of the most important things I can teach you in this book. ☞

☞ **CAN YOU BE PRESIDENT?** If you were born in the United States and are at least thirty-five years old, you can be president. It doesn't matter if you weigh as much as William Howard Taft (332 pounds) or as little as James Madison (100 pounds). It doesn't matter if you are as tall as Abraham Lincoln, who was six foot four, or as short as James Madison (again!), who was five foot four. It doesn't matter if you're born really rich like Thomas Jefferson or really poor like Ulysses S. Grant. It doesn't matter if you're white like John Adams or black like Barack Obama. It doesn't matter if you're a Unitarian like Millard Fillmore or a Catholic like John F. Kennedy. It doesn't matter if you have a physical disability like Franklin D. Roosevelt (who had polio), an emotional disability like Lincoln (who suffered from depression), or a learning difference like Woodrow Wilson (who was dyslexic). It doesn't matter if you're a man or a woman (even though there hasn't been a woman president . . . *yet*). In other words, it doesn't matter whether you are black or white; Jewish, Christian, Muslim, Buddhist, Hindu, or atheist; tall or short; fat or skinny; a man or a woman. *You* can grow up to be president.

LEARNING DIFFERENT. Wilson was famous for being really smart. Before he became president of the United States, he had been a professor and then president of Princeton University. And you know what? He had dyslexia, a learning difference that can make reading and writing very hard no matter *how* smart you are. Wilson didn't learn the alphabet until he was nine and could not read until he was twelve years old. See, you can even have a learning difference and become president.

AT LAST! Do you believe that until 1920 women couldn't vote? Even President Wilson thought that was okay until 1918. Finally, he changed his mind and helped pass the Nineteenth Amendment to the Constitution, which gave women "suffrage," or voting rights.

ALL WORK AND NO PLAY? Have you ever said, "I hate school!"? Imagine working in a dirty factory more than ten hours a day, six days a week, doing the same thing over and over for very little money. Millions of children did that until Woodrow Wilson got Congress to pass a law that made it illegal to hire children under fourteen and limited the number of hours older children could work each day. The Supreme Court blocked that law because they thought it should be up to the states to decide how much kids could work. In fact, today's rules about child labor didn't become law until twenty years later—in 1938, when Franklin D. Roosevelt was president.

WOODROW WILSON

"The world must be made safe for democracy."

WOODROW WILSON dreamed of ending war forever. A year after he became president, the Great War began in Europe. By the time it was over, almost every country in the world was fighting. It is now called World War I. Most Americans wanted the Allies (including England and France) to defeat the Central Powers (led by Germany). Wilson tried to keep us out of that war. Then we found out that Germany was trying to get Mexico to attack America, and German submarines began to sink our cargo ships. So, in 1917, we declared war and joined the Allies.

When the war was over in 1918, Wilson wanted everyone to agree on fourteen points, or rules, that he hoped would end war forever. But many of the Allies were more interested in punishing their enemies than in making a permanent peace. After many months of negotiations in Europe, the president finally got most countries to agree with at least *some* of his ideas. One of his most important ideas was to create an organization of free countries from all over the world who promised to try to settle their arguments peacefully instead of going to war. It was called the League of Nations. But after working so hard to get other countries to join, Wilson couldn't get our own Senate to agree! In the end, the United States never became part of the League of Nations.

Wilson had become president in 1913 with high hopes. When his second term was over in 1921, he was very sick and very disappointed. But he shouldn't have been. He not only tried to keep the United States out of a war, he changed the lives of millions of people back home by making banks more stable and protecting workers.

Official portrait by S. Seymour Thomas

PRESIDENT: March 4, 1913–March 4, 1921

BORN: December 28, 1856

WHERE: Staunton, Virginia

DIED: February 3, 1924 (age 67)

SISTERS: Marion, Anne ("Annie")

BROTHER: Joseph

OCCUPATIONS: lawyer, professor, university president, politician

VICE PRESIDENT: Thomas R. Marshall

PARTY: Democratic

NICKNAME: "Schoolmaster in Politics"

WIVES: Ellen Axson Wilson, Edith Galt Wilson

DAUGHTERS: Margaret ("Nistha"), Jessie, Eleanor (all from his first marriage)

PETS: songbirds, sheep (who kept the grass on the White House lawn trimmed), a ram named Old Ike (who chewed tobacco), Puffins the cat, and dogs—including Davie, Mountain Boy, and Bruce

LOOK FOR HIM . . . OR NOT! $100,000 bill (This note is out of circulation but remains legal tender and is used to transfer money between Federal Reserve banks.)

THE REST OF THE STORY. President Wilson had been born in the South and inherited many racist beliefs. As president, he made sure blacks could no longer serve in the civil service (good jobs in government that are usually permanent). Wilson was a historian and a university president, so you'd think he would have known better than to discriminate against people that way.

WARREN G. HARDING

"Less government in business and more business in government."

Official portrait by Edmund Hodgson Smart

PRESIDENT: March 4, 1921–August 2, 1923

BORN: November 2, 1865

WHERE: Blooming Grove, Ohio

DIED: August 2, 1923 (age 57)

SISTERS: Charity, Mary, Phoebe ("Carolyn"). Two other sisters, Eleanor and Abigail ("Daisy"), died in childhood.

BROTHERS: George. Another brother, Charles, died in childhood.

OCCUPATIONS: newspaper editor and publisher, politician

VICE PRESIDENT: Calvin Coolidge

PARTY: Republican

WIFE: Florence Kling Harding

STEPSON: Marshall ("Pete")

PETS: Pete the squirrel; an English bulldog, Old Boy; canaries; and an Airedale terrier, Laddie Boy

Who was the worst president? Many people say WARREN G. HARDING. But just as I would never say that someone was the best president, I wouldn't say anyone was the worst. I *will* say that Harding may have had the worst friends! To make things even *worse*, he gave them important positions in government.

Several of these "friends" took money (bribes) from companies in exchange for favors. This is called abuse of power, because you are cheating the people who elected you to serve them. It's against the law for any government official to do it.

Even though the president himself might not have broken any laws, he seemed to have some idea of what his friends were up to. But he didn't know how to stop them. (He once said that he knew how to deal with his enemies. It was his friends who kept him awake at night.)

Harding was actually pretty good at doing what the voters elected him to do—get things back to normal after the hard years of World War I. He lowered taxes. He supported the new amendments to the Constitution that gave women the right to vote and made alcohol illegal (although he had plenty of liquor in the White House!).

He signed laws that helped farmers. He signed laws to help big businesses grow faster. He got people excited about new inventions like airplanes and radios.

He also tried to stop the lynching of African Americans. (That's when gangs would capture and hang someone just because of the color of their skin.)

Still, most people only remember what his so-called friends did. He didn't live to see just how much damage they had done. He died of a heart attack in San Francisco, more than a year before his term was up.

READ ALL ABOUT IT. Many presidents are very careful about what they say to the press, but Harding was always very straightforward. Maybe it's because he once owned a newspaper and knew how hard the writers worked to get their facts correct for their stories.

THE TEAPOT DOME SCANDAL. The secretary of the Interior is supposed to take care of all the land that the government owns. During Harding's term, an oil company paid the secretary of the Interior a *lot* of money to let them drill for oil on government lands in Wyoming. (There was a huge rock on those lands that looked like a teapot to some people, so the area was called the "teapot dome.") The secretary was found guilty of taking these bribes and went to jail.

THESE SECRETARIES ARE THE BOSSES. After a president is elected, he or she puts people in charge of different things—for example, working with other countries or making rules for banks and businesses. Those people are called "secretaries" because the president can trust them to keep his plans "secret" until he's ready to talk about them. The problem was that Harding's secretaries kept secrets from *him*.

On August 2, 1923, Vice President CALVIN COOLIDGE was on vacation at his dad's farm in Vermont. The house didn't have any electricity or a phone. At midnight, Coolidge was fast asleep when a messenger arrived with a telegram saying that President Harding had died. Coolidge was now president . . . almost. Every new president has to take the oath of office in front of a judge. Fortunately, his dad was a justice of the peace and, at 2:47 a.m., by the light of an oil lamp, he officially made his own son president. By then the press had gathered and Coolidge gave them a statement. After that he went right back to bed. Seriously!

Like many presidents, Coolidge believed that the best way to make life better for all Americans was to give businesses the help they needed to grow, and let people in different cities and states solve as many of their own problems as possible (instead of having the government do it for them). He thought this because he had grown up in rural Vermont, where people believed everybody should be able to take care of themselves . . . or, when someone couldn't, their neighbors should help them. However, not everyone can grow their own food or cut down trees to build their own houses. And not everyone has neighbors who can help—especially when *everyone* is having a hard time. So his approach did make things very difficult for many poor people. I believe that one of the best things the government can do is help people when their friends and neighbors can't, and America works best when we are all willing to care about other people as much as we care about ourselves. I have a feeling that President Coolidge would have understood that very well.

CALVIN COOLIDGE

"The chief business of the American people is business."

Official portrait by Charles Hopkinson

PRESIDENT: August 2, 1923–March 4, 1929

BORN: July 4, 1872 (the only president born on Independence Day!)

WHERE: Plymouth Notch, Vermont

DIED: January 5, 1933 (age 60)

SISTER: Abigail Grace

OCCUPATIONS: lawyer, politician

VICE PRESIDENTS: none in his first term, Charles G. Dawes (in his second term)

PARTY: Republican

NICKNAME: "Silent Cal"

WIFE: Grace Goodhue Coolidge

SONS: John, Calvin (Calvin died from an infected blister he got while playing tennis on the court at the White House. His father was devastated.)

PETS: a veritable zoo, including dogs, cats, birds, a pair of raccoons, a donkey, a bobcat, two lion cubs, a wallaby, a black bear, and even a pygmy hippo!

A MAN OF FEW WORDS. President Coolidge didn't talk very much. One time a young woman said to him, "I just made a bet that I can get you to say more than two words." Coolidge replied, "You lose."

HOW SILENT *WAS* CAL??? Coolidge talked so little that when he announced the big news that he was *not* going to run for a second term, all he did was write the message on strips of paper and hand them to the newspaper people.

SWEET JOB. Coolidge often helped his father out on the family farm when he was growing up. His favorite chore was making maple syrup. (Can you blame him?)

HERBERT HOOVER

"We in America today are nearer to the final triumph over poverty than ever before in the history of any land."

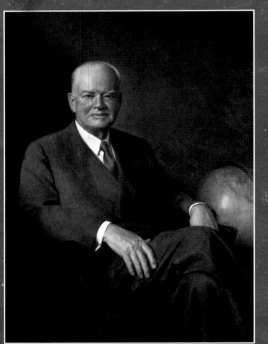

Official portrait by Elmer Wesley Greene

PRESIDENT: March 4, 1929–March 4, 1933

BORN: August 10, 1874

WHERE: West Branch, Iowa

DIED: October 20, 1964 (age 90)

SISTER: Mary ("May")

BROTHER: Theodore ("Tad")

OCCUPATIONS: miner, geologist, engineer, businessman, politician

VICE PRESIDENT: Charles Curtis

PARTY: Republican

WIFE: Lou Henry Hoover

SONS: Herbert Clark, Jr., Allan Henry

PETS: King Tut, Pat, Big Ben, Sonny, Glen, Yukon, Patrick, Eaglehurst Gillette, and Weejie the dogs. Plus two alligators belonging to Allan Henry.

LOOK FOR HIM! Hoover Dam

"HOOVERVILLES." During the Great Depression, many out-of-work people couldn't afford a home and had nowhere to go. So, all over the country, they built little "towns" full of tents and shacks put together with scrap wood. Because some people thought the Depression was Hoover's fault, these towns were called Hoovervilles.

There's a famous expression: "If you find yourself in a hole, stop digging." On October 29, 1929, the country found itself in a *really* deep hole, and no matter how hard the new president, **HERBERT HOOVER**, tried, it just seemed to get deeper.

The hole was the Great Depression. Millions of workers lost their jobs. Farmers lost their farms. There are famous pictures of people standing in long lines just to get a bowl of soup.

The Depression was *not* President Hoover's fault. He was very smart and worked very hard. After college, he actually got a job in a gold mine, ten long hours a day, seven days a week. But soon he was able to use his college education and experience to become an expert in mining gold. He started a business to help companies figure out the best places to dig mines and how to get the gold out. By the time he was forty, he had become a millionaire. So he tried to use the lessons he had learned in business to make decisions about the country's business.

As we've seen again and again, there are two main ways in which presidents try to solve money problems. Some believe it's best if people in the states find the solutions. Others think the federal government needs to help them. Both ideas work some of the time. Neither works all of the time.

Like Calvin Coolidge, who was president before him, Hoover believed that if the government gave too much help to poor people, they wouldn't work as hard to help themselves. (Like, why would you do your chores if your parents would give you allowance money anyway?) He truly believed that if local communities, businesses, and rich people worked together, "prosperity is just around the corner."

Unfortunately, in this case, it wasn't. And it would take a new president to find a way out of that hole.

DON'T MESS WITH VETS. Veterans of World War I were supposed to get a special bonus twenty-five years after the war ended. But many were so poor during the Depression, they needed the money right away. More than 40,000 marchers, including 17,000 veterans plus their families and friends, marched to Washington and lived in shacks while they tried to convince Congress to give them the bonus sooner. They became known as the "Bonus Army." Hoover ordered the U.S. Army to get them to leave, which made people even madder.

PLAY BALL! To help the president stay in shape, Hoover's doctor created a team sport that's kind of like volleyball, but with a super-heavy ball. They called the game Hoover-Ball, and people still play it today. There are even national championships!

FRANKLIN DELANO ROOSEVELT fought three huge battles in his life and won them all. One was personal. One was national. And the third was worldwide.

The personal battle was with polio, a disease that can make it impossible to use your legs. FDR had to wear special leg braces and could stand or walk only by using crutches or leaning against something like a speaking podium. His sons were particularly good at helping him stand without anyone noticing. Still, he was a strong, active president who was elected for an unprecedented four terms, serving for twelve years—longer than any other U.S. president.

His national battle was against the Great Depression. By the time he became president in March 1933, one out of every four people didn't have a job. Thousands of companies, farms, and banks had gone out of business.

Roosevelt promised Americans a "new deal." The government hired people to work on building projects all over the country. Congress passed laws that helped poor people afford houses and made sure workers were paid fairly. He also created a new program called Social Security, which to this day is how the government makes sure older people have something to live on. (Every working person pays a little bit toward it out of each paycheck while he or she has a job, then gets some back after retirement.) But the most important thing FDR gave people was hope. Then, just as things were starting to get better, FDR had to fight his third and biggest battle of all, the worldwide one.

On December 7, 1941, Japanese airplanes attacked our navy's ships at Pearl Harbor, Hawaii. Suddenly we were right in the middle of World War II. We fought alongside our allies for four years until Germany surrendered on May 7, 1945. Japan surrendered a few months later.

Sadly, FDR died on April 12, 1945—shortly after beginning his fourth term—so he didn't live to see the end of the war. But he and the leaders of other countries had already begun making plans to create an organization called the United Nations, where representatives from countries all over the world could work together to solve their differences. The first official meeting of the United Nations took place on January 10, 1946, and seventy years later, it's still making a major contribution to world peace.

You could say Roosevelt won that battle, too.

MORE THAN THE "PRESIDENT'S WIFE." Before Eleanor Roosevelt became first lady, people expected the president's wife to focus on entertaining at the White House and being by the president's side at important events. Eleanor changed all that. She gave him advice on how to help people during the Great Depression and traveled all over the country to see if his plans were working. She encouraged her husband to hire more women in government, supported African Americans' struggle for equal rights, and fought to find homes for refugees from World War II. Even after FDR died, Eleanor continued to work for peace and equality. She was the first person to chair the United Nations Commission on Human Rights.

IT'S ALL RELATIVE. Franklin Delano Roosevelt was a distant cousin of Teddy Roosevelt, and Eleanor Roosevelt was TR's niece. That might seem strange, but it turns out that many of us are related. I found out a few years ago that I am President Lincoln's fourth cousin! If you study your family tree, you might find you're related to a president, too.

"The only thing we have to fear is fear itself— nameless, unreasoning, unjustified terror which paralyzes needed efforts to convert retreat into advance."

Official portrait by Frank O. Salisbury

PRESIDENT: March 4, 1933–April 12, 1945

BORN: January 30, 1882

WHERE: Hyde Park, New York

DIED: April 12, 1945 (age 63)

BROTHER: a half brother, James ("Rosey")

OCCUPATIONS: lawyer, politician

VICE PRESIDENTS: John Nance Garner, Henry A. Wallace, Harry S. Truman

PARTY: Democratic

NICKNAME: "FDR"

WIFE: Eleanor Roosevelt (Her first name was actually Anna—Eleanor was her middle name.)

DAUGHTER: Anna

SONS: James ("Jimmy"), Elliott, Franklin Jr., John. Another Franklin died in infancy.

PETS: Majora the German shepherd, Meggie the Scottish terrier, Winks the Llewellin setter, Tiny the Old English sheepdog, President the Great Dane, Fala the Scottish terrier, and Elliott's bullmastiff, Blaze

LOOK FOR HIM! 10¢ coin

COULD YOU GET POLIO? Remember those shots the doctor gave you when you were little? One of them was a vaccine that protects you from polio— the disease from which FDR and tens of thousands of people suffered. In 1953, a man named Jonas Salk discovered a vaccine that prevents polio, and almost nobody in the United States has become sick with polio since then.

SHOWING A LITTLE RESPECT. These days, photographers like taking pictures of *everything* presidents do. But back then, news photographers felt that Roosevelt's polio was something private, and they rarely photographed him in a wheelchair. Over the years, people have become more respectful of those with disabilities, a process that may have been greatly helped by the inspirational *ability* of a president who met his challenges head-on!

HARRY S. TRUMAN

"The buck stops here."

Official portrait by Martha Greta Kempton

PRESIDENT: April 12, 1945–January 20, 1953

BORN: May 8, 1884

WHERE: Lamar, Missouri

DIED: December 26, 1972 (age 88)

SISTER: Mary Jane

BROTHER: John Vivian

OCCUPATIONS: railroad timekeeper, farmer, owner of a men's clothing store, politician

VICE PRESIDENT: Alben Barkley

PARTY: Democratic

NICKNAME: "Give 'Em Hell Harry"

WIFE: Elizabeth Virginia ("Bess") Wallace Truman

DAUGHTER: Margaret

PETS: a cocker spaniel named Feller (Margaret had an Irish setter named Mike.)

HARRY SET HIS SIGHTS ON THE ARMY! Truman wanted to go to West Point, the prestigious military academy, but was turned down because of his poor eyesight. So he decided to join the National Guard. They also turned him down at first, so he secretly memorized the eye chart, tried again, and passed the test.

HARRY TRUMAN

HARRY TRUMAN became vice president in January 1945, and president just a few months later when Franklin Delano Roosevelt died. Even though FDR had been stricken with polio decades earlier, everyone was surprised by his death. Even Truman wasn't sure he could do the job. He told reporters, "I felt like the moon, the stars, and all the planets had fallen on me."

World War II was finally ending. Germany surrendered on May 7, 1945. But Japan refused to give up. So President Truman had to make a historic decision. Since early in the war, American scientists had been working on a top-secret weapon, a new bomb that was so powerful it could destroy a whole city. It was called the atom bomb, and he wanted to get one before our enemies did. On August 6, 1945, Truman sent an American B-29 bomber to drop an atom bomb on the Japanese city of Hiroshima. Three days later, he approved dropping a second one on the city of Nagasaki. At last, Japan surrendered. The bombs instantly killed more than 100,000 people, but Truman believed even more Americans and Japanese would have died if the war continued.

Harry Truman did have good preparation for being a president. Although he never went to college, he had been a farmer, and a captain in the National Guard during World War I. After the war, he was a businessman and an active politician. In 1934, he became a senator.

As president, he focused on improving the lives of everyday people—particularly soldiers coming home from the war. He integrated the armed forces and tried to help African Americans in other ways. He wanted to do things that would make sure everyone had a job and a good place to live. He also convinced Congress to provide money for Europe's recovery from the war.

During his second term, Truman helped make treaties with other nations where we promised to protect each other from attacks—particularly by communist nations. For example, he led the United States into the Korean War to protect democratic South Korea from the communist countries of North Korea and China. The idea that America should be willing to defend democratic nations against communism, no matter where in the world they are, is known as the Truman Doctrine.

DEWEY DEFEATS TRUMAN? In 1948, when Truman ran for president, the race was so close that some of the morning papers, which had to be printed and distributed late the night before, incorrectly guessed at the outcome and said that his opponent, Thomas Dewey, had won!

THE AEROBIC PRESIDENT? Every morning Truman woke at 5 a.m. and completed a two-mile walk at military pace (120 steps per minute). Instead of a sweatshirt, he wore a suit and tie.

As Supreme Commander of the Allied Forces, General **DWIGHT DAVID EISENHOWER** was victorious in World War II. As America's commander-in-chief, President Eisenhower did everything he could to make sure a war like that never happened again.

The two most powerful countries after the war were the United States and the Soviet Union. To stay powerful, each wanted as many countries as possible on its side. So every time there was a fight for control inside a smaller country, America and the Soviet Union (and other communist countries, like China) would get involved and take opposite positions. The most famous one was in Korea, but there were also major fights in Hungary, Lebanon, Iraq, Egypt, Vietnam, and other places. Since neither America nor the Soviet Union fought each other directly, it was called the Cold War. Both countries had the atom bomb, so if they *had* gone to war with each other, it would have turned into the "hottest" war in history, World War III—and maybe the end of the world.

President Eisenhower didn't want to go to war. But he wasn't going to abandon America's friends either. Solving these problems took courage and a willingness to compromise. Fortunately, Eisenhower had both.

When he wasn't trying to keep us out of a war, Eisenhower increased the minimum wage, built houses for poor people, and added on to President Roosevelt's groundbreaking Social Security laws. But one of the most important things he did was to start building the Interstate Highway System—41,000 miles of road that made it easier for people to travel long distances and for companies to ship their products.

Overall, I think the most important thing that President Eisenhower showed us is that a soldier can fight for peace as hard as he fights in war.

ROAD WARRIOR. One reason Eisenhower knew that the country could build a system of highways that covered the whole country was that he saw in World War II how quickly American soldiers could build roads and bridges when it really mattered.

DWIGHT DAVID EISENHOWER

"Every gun that is made, every warship launched, every rocket fired signifies, in the final sense, a theft from those who hunger and are not fed, those who are cold and are not clothed."

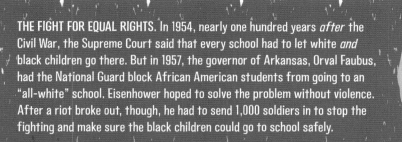

Official portrait by James Anthony Wills

THE FIGHT FOR EQUAL RIGHTS. In 1954, nearly one hundred years *after* the Civil War, the Supreme Court said that every school had to let white *and* black children go there. But in 1957, the governor of Arkansas, Orval Faubus, had the National Guard block African American students from going to an "all-white" school. Eisenhower hoped to solve the problem without violence. After a riot broke out, though, he had to send 1,000 soldiers in to stop the fighting and make sure the black children could go to school safely.

SPACE RACE. One of the biggest "battles" we had with the Soviet Union was to see which country would be the first to put a rocket into outer space. The Soviet Union "won" that battle in 1957. They also were the first to send a man into space, in 1961. But almost a decade later, America "won" the most amazing space race of all: landing men on the moon. Now astronauts from many nations, including the United States and countries in the former Soviet Union, work together on the International Space Station.

STOP CALLING PEOPLE NAMES. The Soviet Union was a group of fifteen communist republics, including Russia. People in communist countries don't have as much freedom as those living in democracies, because the communist government makes far more decisions about what people can say and do. When Eisenhower was president, a few members of Congress started accusing some Americans of being communists and supporting our enemy the Soviet Union—actors, writers, even people serving in the army! Many of these people lost their friends and their jobs because of this name calling, and it caused great division in the country. Kids are often told not to call each other names. Sometimes grown-ups need to learn the same lesson.

PRESIDENT: January 20, 1953–January 20, 1961

BORN: October 14, 1890

WHERE: Denison, Texas

DIED: March 28, 1969 (age 78)

BROTHERS: Arthur, Edgar Newton, Roy, Earl, Milton. Another brother, Paul, died in infancy.

OCCUPATIONS: soldier, five-star U.S. Army general, university president

VICE PRESIDENT: Richard Nixon

PARTY: Republican

NICKNAME: "Ike"

WIFE: Mamie Geneva Doud Eisenhower

SON: John. Another son, Doud ("Icky"), died when he was three.

PETS: a Weimaraner called Heidi and Gabby the parakeet (who is buried on the White House grounds)

JOHN FITZGERALD KENNEDY

"Ask not what your country can do for you—ask what you can do for your country."

Official portrait by Aaron Shikler

PRESIDENT: January 20, 1961–November 22, 1963

BORN: May 29, 1917

WHERE: Brookline, Massachusetts

DIED: November 22, 1963 (age 46)

SISTERS: Rose Marie, Kathleen, Eunice, Patricia, Jean Ann

BROTHERS: Joseph ("Joe"), Robert ("Bobby"), Edward ("Ted")

OCCUPATIONS: writer, U.S. Navy sailor, politician

VICE PRESIDENT: Lyndon B. Johnson

PARTY: Democratic

NICKNAME: "JFK"

WIFE: Jacqueline Bouvier Kennedy

DAUGHTER: Caroline

SONS: John Jr. ("John-John"). Another son, Patrick, died in infancy.

PETS: dogs; birds; two hamsters; a cat; Zsa Zsa the rabbit; Jackie's horse, Sardar; and ponies Macaroni, Tex, and Leprechaun

On November 22, 1963, I walked home from school for lunch. When I opened the door, I heard the phone ringing. It was a friend of my dad's. He told me that President **JOHN F. KENNEDY** had been assassinated.

Just about everyone in my generation can tell you where they were when they heard this news. Kennedy had made us so hopeful about the future. He promised we'd put a man on the moon. He created a Peace Corps of Americans to help people in developing countries do things like build schools and hospitals. He wanted to feed the poor; he wanted black Americans to have the same rights as everyone else; he wanted more people to go to college. Plus, he had been a war hero; he had a beautiful wife and two little kids; he even loved to play touch football! The president, killed? It didn't make any sense. It *still* doesn't make any sense—especially because even today nobody knows for sure why Lee Harvey Oswald, the man who killed Kennedy, did it.

Fortunately, many of JFK's ideas became reality after he died. But one of the most important things he did while still alive was to stand up to the Soviet Union. America was having a *lot* of arguments with them back then. The worst was about Cuba—the only country near us that was communist, like the Soviet Union. In October 1962, we found out that the Soviet Union had moved missiles to Cuba—just ninety miles from our shores. We demanded that they remove them. After many tense conversations between our government and the Soviets, war was avoided . . . but only barely. After that, the two countries began to talk about maybe not building any more nuclear weapons. But there are still more than enough today to destroy every country in the world.

Many historians continue to wonder how things would have been different—in America and the world—if President Kennedy had lived.

IT'S NOT ABOUT RELIGION. Many voters thought it was a problem that John F. Kennedy was a Catholic. They were afraid his religious beliefs would affect his decisions. He told them his religion wasn't a problem. The *real* problem was that America had too many hungry children, not enough schools, and too many people who couldn't afford doctors.

TWENTY-FIVE MILES OF BARBED WIRE . . . After World War II, Berlin, the capital of Germany, was divided in two. East Berlin was almost totally controlled by the Soviet Union. To stop people from trying to escape, the Soviet Union built a twenty-five-mile cinder-block wall with barbed wire on top. But walls and barbed wire can't keep people from wanting to be free. And after nearly thirty years, the Berlin Wall finally came down . . . but more about that later.

THE POWER OF TELEVISION. The first time candidates for president ever debated on TV was when Kennedy ran against Richard Nixon in 1960. People who watched thought Kennedy won the debate. People who listened on radio thought Nixon won. It ended up being one of the closest elections in history—and TV might have made the difference.

"I HAVE A DREAM . . ." On August 28, 1963, the famous civil rights activist Martin Luther King, Jr., gave a speech with the stirring phrase "I have a dream . . ." His dream was that people would all be treated equally. In July 1964, Lyndon Johnson signed the Civil Rights Act of 1964, which made it a law that everybody be given the same opportunities as everyone else, particularly in terms of getting a job or going to school. This important law made it illegal for employers to refuse to hire someone—or for schools to refuse to admit someone—based on the person's race, color, sex, nationality, or religion. It also made it perfectly clear that *every* citizen of voting age must be allowed to vote. Unfortunately, many of Martin Luther King's dreams of equality have not completely come true yet. But the Civil Rights Act was a major step forward.

HOW DID HE DO IT? President Johnson was tall (6'4") and tough. He would grab members of Congress by the lapels and talk real loudly right into their faces until they agreed to vote for his bills. He called it his "power of persuasion." Other people just called him a bully!

WHAT'S A LANDSLIDE? When someone wins an election by a *lot*, it's called a landslide. When Johnson ran for the Senate in 1948, he won by just eighty-seven votes. Some people accused his side of cheating, so they sarcastically called him "Landslide Johnson." But when he ran for president in 1964, he won 61 percent of the vote, which really *was* a landslide.

A PICTURE TELLS A MILLION WORDS. One of the most famous pictures in American history (you can look it up) is of Johnson being sworn in as president on the presidential airplane, Air Force One, just two hours after John F. Kennedy's assassination. Lyndon Johnson's wife is on his right, and President Kennedy's widow, Jacqueline, is on his left. Take a look at that picture sometime and just imagine what they were all feeling.

LYNDON BAINES JOHNSON

36

"We are one nation and one people. Our fate as a nation and our future as a people rest not upon one citizen, but upon all citizens."

Official portrait by Elizabeth Shoumatoff

In a way, history hasn't been fair to **LYNDON B. JOHNSON**, who became president when Kennedy was shot. He isn't always given credit for the many things he did to make America a better place. And he is often blamed for a war he didn't start.

There was a "war" Johnson did start. He called on America to declare a "War on Poverty" and help him create the "Great Society." Many laws he signed are still helping people, including laws to feed the hungry (food stamps); give old, poor, disabled, and very sick people free or low-cost health care (Medicare and Medicaid); improve education (Head Start); and fight discrimination (civil rights). President Kennedy *did* have some of these ideas first, but Johnson was the president who convinced Congress to pass them.

The war many people blame Johnson for began in the 1950s when Presidents Truman and Eisenhower sent financial aid and a few American military advisers to help a small country that came to be called South Vietnam protect itself from a communist uprising. Why did we care about a country thousands of miles away? The simplest answer is that China and the Soviet Union were big supporters of communist North Vietnam, and many Americans were afraid that if we let South Vietnam lose to North Vietnam, the rest of the countries in the region would "fall like dominoes" to communism. That idea became known as the "domino theory."

By 1968, no matter how many troops and weapons Johnson sent to Vietnam or how many laws he got passed to help the poor here in America, it seemed we weren't winning the war in Vietnam or the War on Poverty.

Then, suddenly, Americans had to deal with two historic tragedies. In April, Martin Luther King, Jr., a major leader of the civil rights movement, was assassinated. In June, Robert Kennedy (President Kennedy's younger brother and a senator from New York) was assassinated while running for president. I was only fourteen years old but, along with many Americans, I remember feeling like my country was falling apart.

PRESIDENT: November 22, 1963–January 20, 1969

BORN: August 27, 1908

WHERE: Stonewall, Texas

DIED: January 22, 1973 (age 64)

SISTERS: Rebekah, Josefa, Lucia

BROTHER: Sam

OCCUPATIONS: teacher, politician

VICE PRESIDENTS: none in his first term, Hubert Humphrey (in his second term)

PARTY: Democratic

NICKNAME: "LBJ"

WIFE: Claudia ("Lady Bird") Taylor Johnson

DAUGHTERS: Lynda, Luci

PETS: Blanco the collie, Yuki the mutt, as well as Edgar, Him, Her, and Freckles—all beagles. There were also hamsters and lovebirds.

37 RICHARD M. NIXON

"Always remember, others may hate you. But those who hate you don't win unless you hate them. And then you destroy yourself."

Official portrait by James Anthony Wills

PRESIDENT: January 20, 1969–August 9, 1974

BORN: January 9, 1913

WHERE: Yorba Linda, California

DIED: April 22, 1994 (age 81)

BROTHERS: Edward, Harold, Donald, Arthur

OCCUPATIONS: lawyer, U.S. Navy sailor, politician

VICE PRESIDENTS: Spiro Agnew, Gerald Ford

PARTY: Republican

WIFE: Thelma ("Pat") Ryan Nixon

DAUGHTERS: Patricia ("Tricia"), Julie

PETS: As vice president, Nixon had a famous cocker spaniel, Checkers. When he was in office, there were Vicky the poodle, Pasha the terrier, and King Timahoe the Irish setter.

EQUAL RIGHTS FOR WOMEN STUDENTS. In 1972, Richard Nixon signed a law that is known as Title IX. It said that schools that received money from the government had to let women go to the same classes as men and that women's sports had to be supported as much as men's. (Can you believe it wasn't always that way?)

MY FIRST VOTE. The Twenty-Sixth Amendment to the U.S. Constitution gave eighteen-year-olds the right to vote. It was passed in 1971, which is the year I turned eighteen. So I was able to vote in the 1972 presidential election between Richard Nixon and George McGovern. It meant a lot to me to be able to vote in an election with so many issues that were important to my generation—in particular, the war in Vietnam. I voted in Massachusetts, which is the *only* state Nixon lost.

EARLY TO RISE. When Richard Nixon was a high school kid, he had to wake up at 4 a.m. daily and drive a truck to Los Angeles to buy vegetables for his family's grocery store. Then he'd drive back, wash them, and put them out for sale . . . all before school.

Imagine that you were president when an American first landed on the moon, and you got Congress to pass laws to help the environment, *and* you made friends with one of our biggest enemies (China). Sounds pretty good, right? Well, that's what it was like to be **RICHARD NIXON**.

But wait! Imagine that you were president when many people were out of work and the prices for everything were rising fast, *and* when four college students were killed during a protest against the Vietnam War. Then you were accused of crimes so serious that you became the first president ever to resign. Sounds pretty bad, doesn't it? Well, that's what it was like to be Richard Nixon.

Nixon did many good things as president. He got the voting age lowered to eighteen, began to end the war in Vietnam, launched a "War on Cancer," and opposed discrimination against everyone—from female high school and college students to Native Americans.

But many people remember him best for something that happened on June 17, 1972, when five men broke into the headquarters of the Democratic Party at the Watergate office building in Washington, D.C., and tried to tap the phones so they could listen in on the Democrats' plans for the upcoming presidential election. While it was never proven that Nixon (who was a Republican) told the men to do it, it was clear he tried to cover up the crime . . . so he resigned before he could be impeached. People refer to the event as simply "Watergate." The experience made many people question the honesty of all politicians and, even today, Americans don't trust government the way they did before it happened. It is one of the most famous scandals in American history.

A TRUE FRIEND. President Ford was a star football player at the University of Michigan in the 1930s. His roommate was also a star: a black player named Willis Ward. One time a Southern team said they wouldn't play against a team with a black player. When Michigan agreed to keep Ward from playing, Ford threatened to quit. But Ward insisted that his friend play anyway. Michigan won the game, and Ford told Ward they'd won it for him.

PRESIDENTS CAN BE CLUMSY, TOO! Gerald Ford might have been a talented football player, but he was not always so graceful off the field. While in office, he fell down plane steps, tripped over carpets, and became the subject of some jokes. Even *he* made fun of how clumsy he was! YouTube it!

GERALD R. FORD

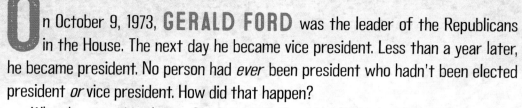

"My fellow Americans, our long national nightmare is over."

On October 9, 1973, GERALD FORD was the leader of the Republicans in the House. The next day he became vice president. Less than a year later, he became president. No person had *ever* been president who hadn't been elected president *or* vice president. How did that happen?

What happened is that in October 1973, President Nixon's vice president, Spiro Agnew, resigned after being accused of several crimes. So Nixon had to choose a new vice president and get Congress to agree. Gerald Ford seemed like a good choice because both Democrats and Republicans liked him. Then, on August 9, 1974, *Nixon* resigned because *he* was accused of serious crimes, so Gerald Ford was suddenly president.

One of the first things President Ford did was pardon former president Nixon. Presidents and governors are able to "pardon" people who are convicted (or even just accused) of a crime when they think there is a special reason to forgive them. President Ford pardoned Richard Nixon before any charges were brought, because he wanted the country to stop focusing on the past and, instead, look to the future. He thought it was the best way to end what he called "our long national nightmare." But it upset many people—especially Democrats, who didn't want to cooperate with the man who they felt had let Nixon "off the hook." Ford even had trouble getting some Republicans to work with him, because they wanted the government to give less assistance to the poor and stop making so many rules for businesses.

Then North Vietnam had a final victory over South Vietnam, and Americans watched on TV as our former allies, the South Vietnamese people, tried desperately to escape. No matter what anyone said, it seemed like the United States had lost the war as much as the South Vietnamese.

Overall, Ford found himself in a lot of no-win situations while he was president. But though many disagreed with him, he never lost the respect of the American people at a time when Americans really needed a president they could trust.

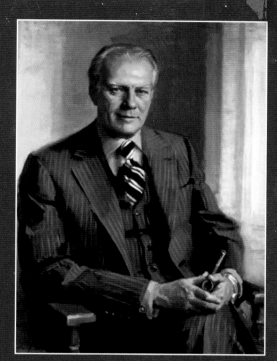

Official portrait by Everett Raymond Kinstler

PRESIDENT: August 9, 1974–January 20, 1977

BORN: July 14, 1913

WHERE: Omaha, Nebraska

DIED: December 26, 2006 (age 93)

HALF SISTERS: Marjorie, Patricia

HALF BROTHERS: Leslie ("Bud") Thomas, Richard, James

OCCUPATIONS: male model, U.S. Navy sailor, lawyer, politician

VICE PRESIDENT: Nelson Rockefeller

PARTY: Republican

NICKNAME: "Jerry"

WIFE: Elizabeth Ann ("Betty") Bloomer Ford

DAUGHTER: Susan

SONS: Michael, John, Steven

PETS: Liberty and Misty, both golden retrievers; another dog, named Lucky; and Shan the Siamese cat

HELPING OUT THE NEXT GUY. When you start a new job, it can really help to get advice from people who have done that job before. Well, there aren't many people who have been president before! So even after Jimmy Carter defeated Gerald Ford in the 1976 election, he would sometimes ask Ford for his opinions about current events. Soon they became close friends.

39

JAMES EARL CARTER, JR.

"Human rights is the soul of our foreign policy."

Official portrait by Herbert Abrams

PRESIDENT: January 20, 1977–January 20, 1981

BORN: October 1, 1924

WHERE: Plains, Georgia

BROTHER: William ("Billy")

OCCUPATIONS: U.S. Navy sailor, farmer, writer, politician, professor, activist

VICE PRESIDENT: Walter Mondale

PARTY: Democratic

NICKNAME: "Jimmy"

WIFE: Eleanor Rosalynn Smith Carter

SONS: John, James III ("Chip"), Donnell ("Jeff")

DAUGHTER: Amy

PETS: dogs Grits and Lewis Brown; and Misty Malarky Ying Yang, a Siamese cat

There's never an easy time to become president. From the very first day, you face huge challenges. President **JIMMY CARTER** had more than his share. One of the hardest was that the prices of gas and oil had almost doubled just before he took office. Remember, we don't just use gas and oil to drive our cars and heat our homes. We also use them to power our factories and farms and to ship everything they make and grow. So when gas and oil prices go up, the price of *everything* goes up. No matter what Carter tried, he couldn't get those prices to go down.

Jimmy Carter's most famous success and failure both happened in the Middle East. The success was helping Israel and Egypt—who had been enemies for many years—sign a peace treaty. The failure happened in late 1979, when dozens of people were taken hostage (captured) at the American embassy in Iran. Fifty-two of them were held for 444 days and weren't released until after Carter lost the election of 1980.

Some historians say Jimmy Carter has been the best ex-president in history. That doesn't mean he was a bad president. It means that he continued to do a lot for people *after* leaving office. He's taught college, written books, and played a major role in Habitat for Humanity, an organization that builds houses for poor people. He also created the Carter Center, which works to protect human rights around the world. Jimmy Carter has proven that being president is just *one* way to make a big difference.

SOLAR-POWERED PRESIDENCY. When gas and oil prices went up, Jimmy Carter encouraged people to drive less, and he lowered the speed limit on highways to 55 miles per hour—both of which saved a lot of gasoline. He also encouraged people to lower the temperature in their homes—and practiced what he preached by lowering the temperature in the White House! He knew those things didn't make him popular, but he also knew that it was important to start finding ways to use less energy. In fact, he was the first president to have solar panels installed on the White House roof—thirty-two in all!

HE EARNED MORE THAN PEANUTS. Jimmy Carter grew up on a big peanut farm in Georgia with no electricity or running water. By the time he was ten, he was loading food onto a wagon and bringing it into town to sell. He saved so much money that when he was only a teenager, he found a way to buy five houses in town and rent them to make money!

A VERY FAMOUS HANDSHAKE. The peace treaty between Egypt and Israel was announced to the world with a picture showing Anwar El Sadat (the president of Egypt), Jimmy Carter, and Menachem Begin (the prime minister of Israel) shaking hands. Sadat and Begin received the Nobel Peace Prize for this important treaty. The prize is given to people who have done something big to make the world a more peaceful place. Years later, President Carter was also awarded the Nobel Peace Prize, for all the good work he did after leaving office.

Presidents are always trying to find a balance between the amount Americans want to pay in taxes (as little as possible!) and what we want the government to do to help us (as much as possible!). Since the more government does, the more it costs, people often talk about "big government" versus "small government."

President RONALD REAGAN believed in small government. That meant he wanted the government to spend less, so people could pay less in taxes. That made things difficult for some poor people as well as businesses that needed to borrow money, because the government wouldn't have the funds to help them. At the same time, his tax cuts helped some other people and businesses, and Reagan believed that, in the long run, making hard choices like this would be best for everyone, including all businesses and the poor.

When it came to defending our country from any possible attack, however, President Reagan was committed to spending whatever it took. In foreign affairs, President Reagan had one big success and made one serious mistake. His success was helping to end the Cold War between the Soviet Union and the United States. By the time he left office, the Soviet Union was near collapse, and many of the countries that were part of it, or had been under its influence, would soon be free. This left us, without question, the strongest country in the world.

Reagan's serious mistake is known as the Iran-Contra affair. Some people who worked with the president developed a complicated plan to free Americans being held hostage. But it involved giving powerful weapons to one of our enemies (Iran) and giving money illegally to the Contras, a group fighting the government in Nicaragua that Congress had specifically voted *not* to give money to. Look up Iran-Contra sometime—it's like reading a spy novel!

Overall, however, Reagan was very popular, even among some Democrats, because of the way he made

RONALD REAGAN

"Government's first duty is to protect the people, not run their lives."

40

Official portrait by Everett Raymond Kinstler

PRESIDENT: January 20, 1981–January 20, 1989

BORN: February 6, 1911

WHERE: Tampico, Illinois

DIED: June 5, 2004 (age 93)

BROTHER: Neil

OCCUPATIONS: actor, broadcaster, Screen Actors Guild president, politician

VICE PRESIDENT: George H. W. Bush

PARTY: Republican

NICKNAMES: "Gipper," "Great Communicator," "Dutch"

WIVES: Jane Wyman, Nancy Davis Reagan

SONS: Michael, Ron

DAUGHTERS: Maureen, Patti. A daughter, Christine, died in infancy.

PETS: Lucky the Bouvier des Flandres, Rex the Cavalier King Charles spaniel, Victory the golden retriever, Peggy the Irish setter, Taca the Siberian husky, Fuzzy the Belgian sheepdog, and horses

HE TALKED THE TALK. President Reagan was called the "Great Communicator" because of his ability to put his opinions into what he called "plain talk" that captured the way many Americans felt—in particular, our hopes for the future. However, he was modest about that talent. He said he was simply expressing "the heart of a great nation."

CALL ME AFTER DINNER. President Reagan and Tip O'Neill, the leader of the Democrats, disagreed about almost everything! Fortunately, they were both very practical and knew how to work together for the good of the country. O'Neill even once said they were friends . . . after 6 p.m.

HE COULD HAVE BEEN A STAR. Actually, when he was younger, Ronald Reagan *was* a movie star. In his most famous film, he played a dying college football player named George Gipp. Some of his last words were "Win just one for the Gipper." Soon the "Gipper" became his nickname.

41 GEORGE H. W. BUSH

"This is America . . . a brilliant diversity spread like stars, like a thousand points of light in a broad and peaceful sky."

1-2-3 JUMP! During World War II, when President Bush was a fighter pilot, his plane was shot down. He parachuted out and survived. Maybe that's why he celebrated his eightieth, eighty-fifth, and, yes, even ninetieth birthdays by making a parachute jump.

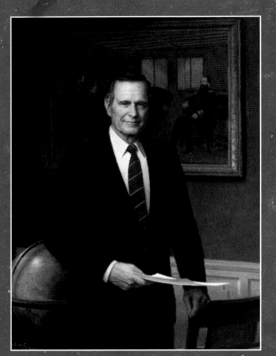

Official portrait by Herbert Abrams

PRESIDENT: January 20, 1989–January 20, 1993

BORN: June 12, 1924

WHERE: Milton, Massachusetts

SISTER: Nancy

BROTHERS: Prescott, Jonathan, William ("Bucky")

OCCUPATIONS: U.S. Navy pilot, businessman, CIA director, ambassador, politician

VICE PRESIDENT: Dan Quayle

PARTY: Republican

NICKNAME: "Poppy"

WIFE: Barbara Pierce Bush

DAUGHTERS: Dorothy ("Doro") and Pauline ("Robin"), who died when she was a child.

SONS: George, John ("Jeb"), Neil, Marvin

PETS: Millie and Ranger, English springer spaniels

Presidents give thousands of speeches. But people usually only remember a few phrases. In his first speech as president, **GEORGE H. W. BUSH** used the phrase "a thousand points of light." His words were poetic, but they were also his attempt to get communities and neighbors to take care of problems the government had been working on for decades. This approach succeeded in some places but not in others . . . especially poorer communities, where people had bigger problems to fix and needed government help to get started.

When Bush became president, the government was losing money. Bush believed that the best way to fix that was for people in cities and states to do more to help each other rather than expecting the federal government to do it. He also asked all Americans to be part of "a kinder, gentler nation"—one of his other famous phrases. It didn't stop the government from losing money, but it was a good reminder that the ways we help each other in our own small communities are as important as what the government does to help us.

The president's biggest challenge overseas happened when Iraq, a country in the Middle East, then led by a dictator named Saddam Hussein, invaded a small country called Kuwait so it could take over the valuable Kuwaiti oil fields. Bush helped assemble an army with soldiers from more than thirty nations (coalition forces) to rescue Kuwait. It was called the Gulf War, and once the coalition launched its big ground attack, Operation Desert Storm, Iraq gave up and left Kuwait in only four days. President Bush could be proud we won that war . . . but getting all those nations to work together was just as big a victory.

HOW DOES AMERICA PAY FOR EVERYTHING? It costs a lot of money to run this country because Americans want to do lots of things—from helping kids go to college to finding a cure for cancer. We also *have* to solve many problems we can't anticipate—from hurricanes to wars. Our taxes pay for some of this. But when people think taxes are too high, the country borrows money, just like people borrow money to buy cars and houses. One of a president's hardest jobs is figuring out how much we should raise in taxes and how much we should borrow.

"READ MY LIPS: NO NEW TAXES." President Bush made that promise when running for president. But later, when Congress said it was time to raise taxes, he agreed. He knew it might make him less popular, but he believed the most important thing was to do what he thought was right for the country.

NO SHOO-IN. Who would you think has the best chance of becoming president after a president has finished his two terms? The vice president, right? Actually, George Bush was one of only *four* vice presidents who have been *elected* right after the president they served under. (The first was John Adams, the second was Thomas Jefferson, and the third was Martin Van Buren.)

THE JAZZ PRESIDENT. President Clinton loves playing the saxophone. He almost became a professional musician instead of a politician. A few times he was able to do both! He played on a TV show while running for president and then again at his inaugural ball.

WILLIAM JEFFERSON CLINTON

"If you live long enough, you'll make mistakes. But if you learn from them, you'll be a better person."

Being president is a juggling act. You can't please everyone all the time. But you can certainly say that **BILL CLINTON** pleased a lot of Americans a lot of the time. The reason is that while he was president, the things people care about most got better: there were more jobs, prices didn't go up much (less inflation), more people owned homes, and schools improved. Clinton even worked with the Republicans to balance the budget! I know that doesn't sound very exciting, but no president had done it in thirty years.

But President Clinton wasn't able to do one thing he and First Lady Hillary Clinton thought would really make a difference for many Americans. They wanted Congress to pass a law that would make sure *everyone* could afford to go to the doctor. To pay for it, there would have had to be a new tax. Congress didn't want to raise taxes, so he wasn't able to get that law passed.

One of the most important things Clinton did was forge an agreement with Mexico and Canada to make it easier for companies to do business in all three countries. He also did quite a bit to encourage other countries to become more democratic, find peaceful ways to resolve conflicts, and protect human rights.

Overall, there was only one *really* bad thing that happened to Clinton. He was accused of lying about something in his personal life. The House of Representatives impeached him for it. That means the House believed he was guilty and wanted the Senate to have a trial to decide. He was found not guilty, apologized to the country, and remained as popular as before.

Official portrait by Simmi Knox

PRESIDENT: January 20, 1993–January 20, 2001

BORN: August 19, 1946

WHERE: Hope, Arkansas

HALF BROTHER: Roger

OCCUPATIONS: lawyer, law professor, politician

VICE PRESIDENT: Al Gore

PARTY: Democratic

NICKNAMES: "Bill," "Bubba"

WIFE: Hillary Rodham Clinton

DAUGHTER: Chelsea

PETS: Socks the cat and Buddy the chocolate Labrador retriever

MAYBE WHEN I GROW UP . . . There's a well-known photograph of Bill Clinton at the White House shaking hands with President Kennedy in 1963. Clinton was just sixteen years old. He was on a trip with a group of other teenagers, who were learning about government. He later said that handshake inspired him to be a politician.

A VERY FAMOUS FIRST LADY. When Bill Clinton was president, one of his most important advisers was his wife, First Lady Hillary Clinton. She was a well-known lawyer who helped him prepare his health care bill. Later she became a U.S. senator and the secretary of state, and has also run for president herself.

GEORGE W. BUSH

"I can hear you! The rest of the world hears you! And the people who knocked these buildings down will hear all of us soon!"

Official portrait by John Howard Sanden

PRESIDENT: January 20, 2001–January 20, 2009

BORN: July 6, 1946

WHERE: New Haven, Connecticut

SISTERS: Dorothy ("Doro"), Pauline ("Robin")

BROTHERS: John ("Jeb"), Neil, Marvin

OCCUPATIONS: baseball team owner, businessman, politician

VICE PRESIDENT: Dick Cheney

PARTY: Republican

NICKNAMES: "W.," "Dubya"

WIFE: Laura Welch Bush

DAUGHTERS: Barbara, Jenna

PETS: Miss Beazley, Spot, and Barney the terriers; India the cat; and Ofelia the longhorn cow that lived at Bush's "western White House" in Texas

September 11, 2001, was one of the saddest days in American history. That morning, terrorists from a group known as al-Qaeda killed the pilots in four airplanes and took over the controls. They crashed two of the planes into the World Trade Center, the two tallest buildings in New York City, and one into the Pentagon in Washington, D.C.—the headquarters of the Department of Defense. A fourth crashed in a field in Pennsylvania after a group of passengers fought back. That plane was believed to be heading for the White House. Altogether, almost 3,000 people died. **GEORGE W. BUSH**, who had only been president a few months, declared a "War on Terror."

President Bush knew from the start that it's really hard to win a war against terrorists because the enemy isn't the army of a country—it's individuals or small groups of people who will do *anything* to hurt people who they think are their enemies. To start fighting back, President Bush ordered an attack on Afghanistan, where Osama bin Laden, the leader of the al-Qaeda terrorists, was hiding from us. Bush also attacked Iraq, led by the dictator Saddam Hussein, because he thought they might be making weapons of mass destruction there and might be giving support to the terrorists. He wasn't able to end the war in Afghanistan. American soldiers defeated Iraq and captured Hussein, but *that* war dragged on and on.

Just before President Bush left office, he faced another huge crisis. Banks and other businesses had been lending too much money to people who couldn't afford to pay it back. Soon these people started losing their homes and savings, and some huge banks and businesses started going bankrupt. President Bush had to convince Congress to lend those companies money so they could stay in business and their employees could keep their jobs.

It was a hard eight years to be president. And things might have been very different for President Bush if not for the day that people now just call 9/11.

EVERY VOTE COUNTS. But was every vote counted? People still argue about who *really* won the presidential election in 2000 between George Bush and Al Gore. Overall, Gore won 543,895 more votes. But because of the rules of the Electoral College (see Grover Cleveland, again!), what mattered was who won the most state votes. The last state to be counted was Florida—and everyone knew that whoever won Florida would win the election. Nearly 6 million people voted in the state, and Bush won by just 537 votes. John Quincy Adams, Rutherford B. Hayes, and Benjamin Harrison also won the presidency without winning the most votes nationwide.

FIELD OF DREAMS. Bush dreamed of being a big-league baseball player when he grew up. That didn't happen, but he did the next-best thing . . . he acquired a team! He was one of the owners of the Texas Rangers, the Major League Baseball team in Arlington, until just before he became governor of Texas and then president.

HAVE TROUBLE READING? Some people think that George Bush, like Woodrow Wilson, has a learning difference called dyslexia that makes it hard to read. It's another example of how *anyone* who tries hard enough can grow up to be president.

LIKE FATHER, LIKE SON. George Walker Bush was the 43rd president. His father, George Herbert Walker Bush, was the 41st. The only other father-son presidents were John Adams and John Quincy Adams, almost 200 years before

YES, THEY COULD! After law school, most people become . . . lawyers! Obama spent two years helping people in poor areas of Chicago, Illinois, instead. Working with the community, he convinced the city to help them do things like build parks and recreation centers designed to make the streets safer for kids.

YOU PROMISED, DAD . . . When Obama was running for president, he promised his daughters, Malia and Sasha, they'd get a puppy to take to the White House if he won. He kept his promise. They adopted a puppy named Bo in 2009. In 2013, Bo got a little sister named Sunny.

HE CAN JUMP! President Obama loves basketball. Sometimes when he visits a school (or military base), he'll go to the gym and shoot a few hoops with the kids (or troops).

LET'S MOVE, KIDS! A lot of kids are overweight these days, which can be really bad for their health. First Lady Michelle Obama created a program called Let's Move! to get kids to eat better and exercise more.

"Yes we can."

44

FIRST AFRICAN AMERICAN PRESIDENT. People often say one of the most important things about Barack Obama is that he was our first African American president. It *was* an amazing step forward for him and the country. But someday a president's gender, race, color, religion, or sexual orientation won't matter at all to voters. *That* will be *really* amazing.

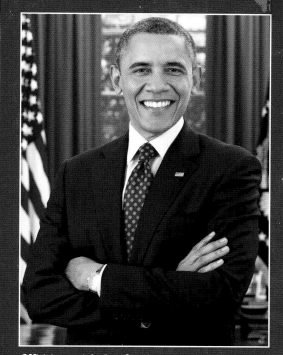

Official portrait by Pete Souza

A t the Democratic Convention in 2004, a young state senator from Illinois gave the keynote speech. It was so powerful and inspiring that it changed his life and the future of the country.

I'm pretty sure you know who gave that speech. His name is **BARACK OBAMA**, and four years later, he became our 44th president. When he became president, the country was in a real fiscal crisis. Many companies were going out of business, and people were losing their jobs. To create jobs as fast as possible, he started government projects that he hoped would help the country now and in the future (like repairing roads and bringing faster Internet to more places). He also continued the program President Bush had started to lend *billions* of dollars to big businesses. This government bailout was very risky and not very popular. But not only did it work, most of the businesses paid back the money.

President Obama is especially proud that he convinced Congress to pass a law so *every* American could afford health care—an idea that had been the dream of many presidents since Theodore Roosevelt.

He is also known for bringing our troops back from the Middle East and ordering a mission in which American soldiers found and killed Osama bin Laden—the man who sent the terrorists to attack America on 9/11.

President Obama signed one law that's really important for *you*. He knew that American students weren't doing as well in school as students in some other countries—especially in math and science. So he created a program called Race to the Top. He did it so *you* can get a better education . . . so *you* can go to college . . . and so *you* can be more successful. Because *you* are the future of America.

PRESIDENT: January 20, 2009–Incumbent

BORN: August 4, 1961

WHERE: Honolulu, Hawaii

HALF SISTERS: Auma, Maya

HALF BROTHERS: Malik ("Roy"), Abo, Bernard, Mark, David, George

OCCUPATIONS: community organizer, lawyer, law professor, politician

VICE PRESIDENT: Joe Biden

PARTY: Democratic

NICKNAME: "No Drama Obama"

WIFE: Michelle Robinson Obama

DAUGHTERS: Malia, Natasha ("Sasha")

PETS: Bo and Sunny the Portuguese water dogs

SELECTED PRESIDENTIAL BIRTHPLACES, LIBRARIES, MUSEUMS, AND HISTORIC SITES

★ ★ ★ ★ ★ ★ ★ ★

ARKANSAS

CLINTON: President William Jefferson Clinton Birthplace Home National Historic Site (President Bill Clinton's 1st Home Museum), Hope, AR

CALIFORNIA

NIXON: Nixon Presidential Library and Museum and Richard M. Nixon Birthplace, Yorba Linda, CA

REAGAN: Ronald Reagan Presidential Library and Museum, Simi Valley, CA

FLORIDA

TRUMAN: Harry S. Truman Little White House, Key West, FL

GEORGIA

F. ROOSEVELT: Roosevelt's Little White House State Historic Site, Warm Springs, GA

CARTER: Jimmy Carter National Historic Site, Plains, GA

ILLINOIS

LINCOLN: Lincoln Home National Historic Site, Springfield, IL

REAGAN: Ronald Reagan Boyhood Home, Dixon, IL

INDIANA

W. HARRISON: William Henry Harrison Home (Grouseland), Vincennes, IN

LINCOLN: Lincoln Boyhood National Memorial, Lincoln City, IN

B. HARRISON: Benjamin Harrison Home, Indianapolis, IN

IOWA

HOOVER: Herbert Hoover National Historic Site, West Branch, IA

KANSAS

EISENHOWER: Dwight D. Eisenhower Presidential Library, Museum, and Boyhood Home, Abilene, KS

KENTUCKY

TAYLOR: Zachary Taylor Home (Springfield), Louisville, KY

LINCOLN: Abraham Lincoln Birthplace National Historical Park, Hodgenville, KY

MARYLAND

NIXON: Nixon Presidential Library, College Park, MD

MASSACHUSETTS

J. ADAMS: Adams National Historical Park, Quincy, MA

J. Q. ADAMS: Adams National Historical Park, Quincy, MA

KENNEDY: John Fitzgerald Kennedy National Historic Site, Brookline, MA

MICHIGAN

FORD: Gerald R. Ford Presidential Library and Museum, Grand Rapids, MI

MISSOURI

GRANT: Ulysses S. Grant National Historic Site (White Haven), St. Louis, MO

TRUMAN: Harry S. Truman National Historic Site, Grandview, MO

NEW HAMPSHIRE

PIERCE: Franklin Pierce Homestead, Hillsborough, NH

NEW JERSEY

CLEVELAND: Grover Cleveland Birthplace State Historic Site, Caldwell, NJ

NEW YORK

VAN BUREN: Martin Van Buren National Historic Site (Lindenwald), Kinderhook, NY

FILLMORE: Millard Fillmore House, East Aurora, NY

GRANT: General Grant National Memorial (Grant's Tomb), New York, NY

ARTHUR: Chester A. Arthur Home, New York, NY

T. ROOSEVELT: Theodore Roosevelt Birthplace National Historic Site, New York, NY

T. ROOSEVELT: Sagamore Hill National Historic Site, Oyster Bay, NY

F. ROOSEVELT: Home of Franklin D. Roosevelt National Historic Site, Hyde Park, NY

NORTH CAROLINA

POLK: President James K. Polk State Historic Site, Pineville, NC

A. JOHNSON: Andrew Johnson Birthplace (Mordecai Historic Park), Raleigh, NC

NORTH DAKOTA

T. ROOSEVELT: Theodore Roosevelt National Park, Medora, ND

OHIO

HAYES: Rutherford B. Hayes Presidential Center (Spiegel Grove), Fremont, OH

GARFIELD: James A. Garfield National Historic Site (Lawnfield), Mentor, OH

McKINLEY: William McKinley Tomb, Canton, OH

TAFT: William Howard Taft National Historic Site, Cincinnati, OH

HARDING: Harding Home, Marion, OH

PENNSYLVANIA

BUCHANAN: James Buchanan House (Wheatland), Lancaster, PA

EISENHOWER: Eisenhower National Historic Site, Gettysburg, PA

SOUTH CAROLINA

JACKSON: Andrew Jackson State Park, Lancaster, SC

WILSON: Thomas Woodrow Wilson Boyhood Home, Columbia, SC

SOUTH DAKOTA

WASHINGTON, JEFFERSON, LINCOLN, T. ROOSEVELT: Mount Rushmore National Memorial, Keystone, SD

TENNESSEE

JACKSON: The Hermitage, Nashville, TN

POLK: James K. Polk Ancestral Home, Columbia, TN

A. JOHNSON: Andrew Johnson National Historic Site, Greeneville, TN

TEXAS

L. JOHNSON: Lyndon B. Johnson National Historical Park, Johnson City, TX

G. BUSH: George Bush Presidential Library and Museum, College Station, TX

G. W. BUSH: George W. Bush Presidential Library and Museum, Dallas, TX

G. W. BUSH: George W. Bush Childhood Home, Midland, TX

VERMONT

ARTHUR: President Chester A. Arthur State Historic Site, Fairfield, VT

COOLIDGE: President Calvin Coolidge State Historic Site (Calvin Coolidge Homestead District), Plymouth, VT

VIRGINIA

WASHINGTON: Mount Vernon, Mount Vernon, VA

JEFFERSON: Monticello, Charlottesville, VA

MADISON: Montpelier, Orange, VA

MONROE: Oak Hill (James Monroe House), Aldie, VA

W. HARRISON: Berkeley Plantation, Charles City, VA

TYLER: John Tyler Home (Sherwood Forest Plantation), Charles City, VA

HOOVER: President Herbert and Lou Henry Hoover's Rapidan Camp, Shenandoah National Park, Syria, VA

WASHINGTON, D.C.

WASHINGTON: Washington Monument

JEFFERSON: Thomas Jefferson Memorial

LINCOLN: Lincoln Memorial

WILSON: Woodrow Wilson House

F. ROOSEVELT: Franklin Delano Roosevelt Memorial

★ ★ ★ ★

AND CHECK THESE OUT, TOO!

Eleanor Roosevelt National Historic Site, Hyde Park, NY

Federal Hall National Memorial, New York, NY

First Ladies National Historic Site, Canton, OH

Independence National Historical Park, Philadelphia, PA

White House, Washington, D.C.

GLOSSARY

★ ★ ★ ★ ★ ★ ★ ★

AMENDMENT: An addition to the United States Constitution. Two good examples are the amendment ending slavery during President Lincoln's term (p. 33) and the one giving women the right to vote while President Wilson was in office (p. 56).

ASSASSINATION: The murder of an important person because of what they did or what they believed. Four American presidents have been assassinated: Lincoln, Garfield, McKinley, and Kennedy.

BILL OF RIGHTS: The first ten amendments to the United States Constitution. These rights include freedom of speech, religion, press, and assembly, and the right to a fair and speedy trial, among others. James Madison (p. 9) proposed the amendments that became the Bill of Rights while serving as a congressman from Virginia.

BRIBE: In politics, a bribe means giving politicians money so they'll offer someone a job, or they'll vote in favor of what the person giving them the bribe wants—not what's good for everyone. (See **GRAFT.**)

CABINET: The heads of all the government departments. Currently there are fifteen departments: Agriculture, the Attorney General, Commerce, Defense, Education, Energy, Health and Human Services, Homeland Security, Housing and Urban Development, Interior, Labor, State, Transportation, Treasury, and Veterans Affairs.

CAPITALISM: A political system in which most businesses and property are owned by individuals or groups of individuals instead of the government. Capitalists believe this system gives everyone a chance to live a better life if they study harder or work harder or come up with exciting new ideas. Of course, it doesn't always work out that way. (See **COMMUNISM.**)

COLONY: A territory under the control of another country. Before they became the United States of America, the original thirteen states were British colonies.

COMMUNISM: A political system in which the government owns nearly everything and tries to make sure that everyone has a job, gets roughly the same amount of food and clothes, and has the same kind of home. Communists believe this system is the best way to make sure everyone has what they need to live, instead of some people being rich and other people being poor. It doesn't work out that way, though. (See **CAPITALISM.**)

CONFEDERACY: The eleven Southern states that seceded from the United States in 1860 and 1861, leading, ultimately, to the Civil War.

CONGRESS: The legislative branch of the United States government. Congress makes the laws. Each state also has its own legislature with two houses (except Nebraska, which has one combined house). (See **LEGISLATIVE BRANCH.**)

CONSERVATIVE: The word *conserve* means "to save or hold on to," and a conservative is a person who is cautious about change—usually preferring to make laws based on traditional beliefs and values rather than trying too many new things. (See **LIBERAL.**) Hardly anyone is liberal or conservative about everything.

CONSTITUTION: The document that describes how the United States government should work. It's like an operating manual for our democracy.

DEMOCRACY: A government system in which the people vote to decide who will be in charge of the things that matter to everyone. This includes voting for the president and Congress, as well as for the people who will be responsible for your schools, city, and state. The United States is a democracy.

DEMOCRATIC PARTY: One of the major political parties in the United States. Generally, Democrats try to find ways for the federal government to help people rather than leaving everything up to business and local communities. The first Democratic president was Andrew Jackson.

DICTATOR: A ruler who has complete power over a country. Instead of being elected, a dictator uses force to take over and remain in power. Even if someone was voted into office, they can *become* a dictator if they refuse to step down when it's time for someone new to take charge.

DISCRIMINATION: Treating people unfairly or differently because of their race, age, sex or sexual preferences, religion, or nationality.

ELECTORAL COLLEGE: The designated group of people (electors) who decide who gets elected president. Usually the same person who wins the most votes in the country gets the most votes in the Electoral College, but that doesn't always happen. (See, for example, p. 48.)

EMANCIPATION: Freeing a group of people. Lincoln's famous Emancipation Proclamation said that the United States should set the slaves free.

EXECUTIVE BRANCH: One of three branches of the United States government. The president is the head of the executive branch, which is responsible for making sure federal laws are enforced. The executive branch includes all the Cabinet departments.

FEDERAL: A type of government in which individual governments (like states) come together to work on many issues, but still have the power to do other things on their own.

FEDERALIST PARTY: America's first political party. Federalists believed in having a strong national government. The Federalist Party no longer exists, but there was one Federalist president. (See p. 4.)

GRAFT: A corrupt act in which a politician uses his office for personal gain. (See **BRIBE.**)

IMMIGRANT: A person who comes from another country. The United States is often called a nation of immigrants because everybody who lives here (except for Native Americans) either came from a different country or can trace their family history back to some other country or countries.

IMPEACHMENT: The process that occurs if the House of Representatives accuses the president of breaking the law while in office. Just like anyone who is accused of a crime, the president is considered innocent until proven guilty at trial. For the president, there is a trial in the Senate to decide if he is guilty. Two presidents have been impeached—President Andrew Johnson and President Bill Clinton—but both were found *not* guilty. President Richard Nixon left office before his impeachment was voted on.

INAUGURATION: The ceremony in which the elected president officially becomes president. On Inauguration Day, the new president recites the oath of office, promising to do the best job he can, based on the Constitution. He usually also gives a speech talking about what he hopes to accomplish during his presidency.

JIM CROW LAWS: Laws that were passed after the Civil War to prevent African Americans from being treated the same as white Americans. Jim Crow laws were passed mostly in the South, in specific towns or even a whole state. Jim Crow was the stage name of a white performer in the 1800s who blackened his face and acted foolishly as a way of making fun of African Americans. Many Jim Crow laws continued to be in effect until President Lyndon Johnson signed the Civil Rights Act of 1964.

JUDICIAL BRANCH: One of three branches of the United States government. The Supreme Court is the head of the judicial branch and works with the other two branches (see **EXECUTIVE BRANCH** and **LEGISLATIVE BRANCH**) to run the country. By creating three branches, the people who wrote the Constitution hoped that no one person or group of people would have too much power. (See p. 44.)

LEGISLATIVE BRANCH: One of three branches of the United States government. Congress makes up the legislative branch, and it works with the executive and judicial branches to create rules and regulations and, of course, pass laws. Congress consists of two houses: the Senate and the House of Representatives. The 100 senators, two from each state, are elected for six years at a time, and the 435 members of the House are elected for two years at a time. The number of House members each state has is based on the number of people in different towns or cities or regions.

LIBERAL: A person who usually believes in being open to new ideas and change. (See **CONSERVATIVE.**) Hardly anyone is liberal or conservative about everything.

PARDON: To forgive someone for a crime they committed. A governor can pardon someone for a crime in a state, but only the president has the power to pardon those convicted of a federal crime. A pardon may be given to someone who hasn't yet been convicted of a crime—or even charged. President Ford granted the most famous presidential pardon. (See p. 77.)

PATRONAGE: Giving someone a job because they're a friend or family member, or have promised or delivered something in return—not necessarily because they deserve it.

RECONSTRUCTION: The period after the Civil War when the country tried to "reconstruct," or put itself back together—in particular, what the government did to improve the lives of former slaves and make the Confederate states part of the United States again.

REPRESENTATIVE: The name for the men and women who serve in the United States House of Representatives. Representatives are also called congressmen and congresswomen. The members of a state house or assembly are called state representatives. Many of our presidents have served in a state legislature, the United States Congress, or both.

REPUBLICAN PARTY: One of the major political parties in the United States. In general, Republicans are more conservative, which means they don't like change as much as Democrats do. They also believe that, as much as possible, individuals and businesses should do the best they can on their own, instead of having the government be more involved. The first Republican president was Abraham Lincoln.

SECRETARY: The president's Cabinet includes fifteen department heads, all called secretaries, except the attorney general. (See **CABINET.**) Being a secretary is a very important job. If a president doesn't have a good Cabinet, it's harder for him to accomplish what he wants to get done. (See p. 59.)

SENATOR: A man or woman who serves in the United States Senate. Every state gets to elect two senators. Since there are fifty states, there are one hundred senators. If the Senate votes on something and the result is a 50–50 tie, the vice president casts the deciding vote. There are also *state* senates, where *state* senators make decisions about more local matters.

SLAVERY: A practice in which people own other people. Many African Americans were slaves until the Civil War. In the Emancipation Proclamation, President Lincoln said slaves should be free (p. 32), but it wasn't until President Lyndon Johnson signed the Civil Rights Act of 1964 (p. 72) that the government promised to protect the rights of all Americans.

SOVIET UNION (USSR): Some people think the Soviet Union is another name for Russia, but that's not true. For most of the twentieth century, Russia, along with some other nations in Eastern Europe and Asia, were unified, often against their will, under a collective communist government and economy called the Union of Soviet Socialist Republics (Soviet Union), or the USSR. At the end of the Cold War, the Soviet Union disbanded, creating a number of independent nations.

STATE: A region in which the people have decided to work together under one government. Sometimes, like in the United States, individual states decide to join together under one "federal," or united, government. (See **FEDERAL.**)

SUFFRAGE: The right to vote in elections. Until the passage of the Nineteenth Amendment in 1920 (p. 56), women didn't have the right to vote. People who fought for that right were called suffragists. The term *suffragist* is often associated with women, but suffrage is about *anyone's* right to vote.

TARIFF: A tax on goods made in the United States but sold outside of the country, or made abroad and brought from other countries to sell here. Making tariffs fair was a particularly big challenge for President Polk (p. 22) and President Benjamin Harrison (p. 47).

TAXES: Money that people pay to the United States, states, cities, and/or towns. Taxes can be based on how much money people make, what property they own, or how much they spend buying things. Governments use money from taxes to pay for schools, roads, and bridges, as well as the military, government employees, and programs to help people and businesses.

TERRITORY: An area of land that has not yet been declared a state or part of one. For a territory to become a state, the president, Congress, and people in the territory have to agree. (See p. 25.)

TREASURY: The Department of the Treasury takes care of the government's money. It is responsible for printing money, and includes the Internal Revenue Service (IRS), which raises money for the government by collecting taxes.

TREATY: An official agreement among countries.

UNION: To *unite* means "to bring together." That's why the Union was the name used during the Civil War period to describe the states that continued to stay together as the United States while fighting against the Confederacy, which wanted to be a separate country.

VETO: The president can reject a decision or law approved by Congress by vetoing it. Some presidents have used their veto power a lot more than others. (See pp. 14 and 45.) Congress can override a veto, but it takes more members than it did to pass the law in the first place.

WHIG PARTY: An early political party in the United States. Formed in opposition to President Andrew Jackson in 1833, Whigs believed that America should be more progressive, and that Congress should be more important than the president. There were four Whig presidents before the party lost support: William Henry Harrison, John Tyler (who actually didn't really get along with the party), Zachary Taylor, and Millard Fillmore.

ACKNOWLEDGMENTS

Books are often a solitary endeavor, but this one was gloriously collaborative and requires a number of important acknowledgments and profound thank-yous. From my end of things, this book would have long ago foundered if not for the signal contributions of David Blistein and Cauley Powell. David, my oldest friend and alter ego, shepherded along the text with his unique humor and sensitivity. Cauley organized everything else, keeping us on schedule, coordinating the complicated process of midwifing this book from a good idea to something you're holding in your hand. She was indefatigable—and indispensable. Profound thanks also go to Tim Brennan, a great artist and patient friend, who worked on the original conception of this book. Others from Florentine Films who graciously helped are Elle Carrière, Christopher Darling, and Nicole Bevans.

My agent, Jay Mandel, kindly led us to Random House, where we have taken advantage of the talents of a supremely gifted team that includes Michelle Frey, Katrina Damkoehler, Dominique Cimina, and Kelly Delaney, along with Artie Bennett, Alison Kolani, Carol Naughton, Nancy Hinkel, Jenny Brown, and Barbara Marcus.

Bernard Weisberger, William Leuchtenburg, and Geoffrey C. Ward, three of this country's most distinguished historians, answered our questions and read (and reread) our text, giving us invaluable suggestions and saving us from embarrassing errors. Bernie also wrote extensive thumbnail biographies for all the presidents, which formed the basis of our initial writing.

This book would not exist without the sublime gifts and expansive visual wisdom of our illustrator, Gerald Kelley. He "got" what we were trying to do and breathed incredible life into the complicated human beings who have occupied the highest office in the land. We are so grateful—and lucky—to have worked with him.

Finally, work of any kind removes me from my family, and this project was no exception. So I am especially grateful to my wife, Julie; our daughters, Olivia and Willa; not to mention my grown daughters, Sarah and Lilly; for their support and forbearance. They are *all* my inspiration.